The Distributional Impacts of Trade

TRADE AND DEVELOPMENT SERIES

The Distributional Impacts of Trade

Empirical Innovations, Analytical Tools, and Policy Responses

Jakob Engel, Deeksha Kokas, Gladys Lopez-Acevedo, and Maryla Maliszewska

Titles in the Trade and Development Series

The Trade and Development series seeks to provide objective, accessible information about the new trade agenda. Titles in the series cover a wide range of topics, from regional trade agreements and customs reform to agriculture, intellectual property rights, services, and other key issues currently being discussed in World Trade Organization negotiations. Contributors to the series represent some of the world's leading thinkers and specialists on international trade issues.

The Distributional Impacts of Trade: Empirical Innovations, Analytical Tools, and Policy Responses (2021) by Jakob Engel, Deeksha Kokas, Gladys Lopez-Acevedo, and Maryla Maliszewska

A Step Ahead: Competition Policy for Shared Prosperity and Inclusive Growth (2017) by World Bank

Making Global Value Chains Work for Development (2016) by Daria Taglioni and Deborah Winkler

Valuing Services in Trade: A Toolkit for Competitiveness Diagnostics (2015) by Sebastián Sáez, Daria Taglioni, Erik van der Marel, Claire H. Hollweg, and Veronika Zavacka

Trade and Transport Corridor Management Toolkit (2014) by Charles Kunaka and Robin Carruthers

Regulatory *Assessment Toolkit: A Practical Methodology for Assessing Regulation on Trade and Investment in Services* (2014) by Martín Molinuevo and Sebástian Sáez

Trade Competitiveness Diagnostic Toolkit (2012) by Jose Guilherme Reis and Thomas Farole

Exporting Services: A Developing Country Perspective (2011) by Arti Grover Goswami, Aaditya Mattoo, and Sebastián Sáez

Preferential Trade Agreement Policies for Development: A Handbook (2011) by Jean-Pierre Chauffour and Jean-Christophe Maur

Trade Finance during the Great Trade Collapse (2011) by Jean-Pierre Chauffour and Mariem Malouche

Managing Openness: Trade and Outward-oriented Growth After the Crisis (2011) by Mona Haddad and Ben Shepherd

Global Value Chains in a Postcrisis World: A Development Perspective (2010) by Olivier Cattaneo, Gary Gereffi, and Cornelia Staritz

International Trade in Services: New Trends and Opportunities for Developing Countries (2010) by Olivier Cattaneo, Michael Engman, Sebastián Sáez, and Robert M. Stern

Agricultural Price Distortions, Inequality, and Poverty (2010) by Kym Anderson, John Cockburn, and Will Martin

Distortions to Agricultural Incentives: A Global Perspective, 1955-2007 (2009) by Kym Anderson

Trade Preference Erosion: Measurement and Policy Response (2009) by Bernard M. Hoekman, Will Martin, and Carlos Alberto Primo Braga

Distortions to Agricultural Incentives in Africa (2009) by Kym Anderson and William A. Masters

Distortions to Agricultural Incentives in Asia (2009) by Kym Anderson and Will Martin

Distortions to Agricultural Incentives in Europe's Transition Economies (2008) by Kym Anderson and Johan Swinnen

Distortions to Agricultural Incentives in Latin America (2008) by Kym Anderson and Alberto Valdés

The International Migration of Women (2007) by Maurice Schiff, Andrew R. Morrison, and Mirja Sjöblom

International Migration, Economic Development and Policy (2007) by Maurice Schiff and Çağlar Özden

Services Trade and Development: The Experience of Zambia (2007) by Aaditya Mattoo and Lucy Payton

Global Integration and Technology Transfer (2006) by Bernard M. Hoekman and Beata Smarzynska Javorcik

Poverty and the WTO: Impacts of the Doha Development Agenda (2006) by Thomas W. Hertel and L. Alan Winters

Safeguards and Antidumping in Latin America Trade Liberalization: Fighting Fire with Fire (2005) by J. Michael Finger and Julio J. Nogués

Economic Development and Multilateral Trade Cooperation (2005) by Bernard M. Hoekman and Simon J. Evenett

Agricultural Trade Reform and the Doha Development Agenda (2005) by Kym Anderson and Will Martin

International Migration, Remittances, and the Brain Drain (2005) by Maurice Schiff and Çağlar Özden

International Trade in Health Services and the GATS: Current Issues and Debates (2005) by Chantal Blouin, Nick Drager, and Richard Smith

Turkey: Economic Reform and Accession to the European Union (2005) by Bernard M. Hoekman and Sübidey Togan

Customs Modernization Handbook (2005) by Luc De Wulf and José B. Sokol

Intellectual Property and Development: Lessons from Recent Economic Research (2005) by Keith E. Maskus and Carsten Fink

Customs Modernization Initiatives: Case Studies (2004) by Luc De Wulf and José B. Sokol

China and the WTO: Accession, Policy Reform, and Poverty Reduction Strategies (2004) by Deepak Bhattasali, Shantong Li, and Will Martin

Agriculture and the WTO: Creating a Trading System for Development (2004) by Merlinda Ingco and John D. Nash

Poor People's Knowledge: Promoting Intellectual Property in Developing Countries (2004) by J. Michael Finger and Philip Schuler

East *Asia Integrates: A Trade Policy Agenda for Shared Growth* (2004) by Kathie Krumm and Homi Kharas

Domestic Regulation and Service Trade Liberalization (2003) by Pierre Sauve and Aaditya Mattoo

Moving People to Deliver Services (2003) by Aaditya Mattoo and Antonia Carzaniga

India and the WTO (2003) by Aaditya Mattoo and Robert M. Stern

All books in the Trade and Development series are available for free at https://open-knowledge.worldbank.org/handle/10986/2173.

Contents

Boxes

Figures

Map

Tables

Foreword

The last several years have exposed deep divisions over the impact of global trade. These divergent perceptions have increasingly impacted trade policies, and some countries that have traditionally been at the center of the multilateral trading system have retreated.

At the heart of the tensions between trade's supporters and detractors is the fact that the gains from trade accrue unequally among countries and among different groups, sectors, and regions within countries. If trade is to remain a source of growth and poverty reduction, understanding why gains from trade are distributed as they are is critical.

But we must be clear from the start: the relationship between trade and growth is unequivocal. Trading nations have created new markets for their goods, increased the productivity of their workers, and gained skills and knowledge from their trading partners. In the past few decades, the positive role of trade has been further entrenched through its correlation with poverty reduction. From 1990 to 2017, global extreme poverty fell from 36 to 9 percent, while developing countries increased their share in global exports from 16 to 30 percent.

But while the aggregate gains from trade are clearly established, a burgeoning literature within economics has shown that the losses from trade may be deeper, more concentrated, and longer-lasting than previously understood. This literature, however, has been focused primarily on advanced economies.

Global trade will play a critical role in driving economic recovery from the COVID-19 pandemic; ensuring the flow of food, medical supplies, and vaccines; and helping to further reduce poverty. This makes it all the more important to better understand and communicate the relationship between trade and welfare across populations, as well as its role in reducing global disparities.

This report offers a detailed perspective on how the gains from trade may differ across regions, industries, and demographic groups in developing countries. Because good jobs are scarce in these economies, the focus is on expanding and broadening the employment opportunities created through trade. In contrast, the loss of existing good jobs that has been documented in advanced countries is typically less relevant. The report provides new knowledge, data, and tools to inform policy responses to spread the gains from trade more widely and to make trade work for everyone.

Importantly, the analysis shows that countries should continue seeing trade as a pathway to development. The evidence remains strong that trade leads to higher growth and better jobs.

But the report also shows where previous analysis may have fallen short and provides new resources and actionable guidance for policy makers to ensure greater gains from trade while minimizing the losses. Specifically, in extending the latest economic thinking to developing countries through a series of newly developed models and databases and five country case studies, the report aims to help trade policy makers better identify who will benefit and who may need support as the structure of the economy changes through trade.

In line with the World Bank Group's Green, Resilient, and Inclusive Development (GRID) approach, the report highlights a better way forward to help maximize the gains from trade and support lasting and inclusive economic growth, in turn restoring momentum to the United Nations' Sustainable Development Goals.

Among the most critical lessons of the report is that maximizing the gains from trade requires a comprehensive and economy-wide approach. This includes understanding how to facilitate labor mobility as well as the importance of complementary policies, such as business environment reforms and supporting skills development. Developing countries can use the analysis, data, and tools in the report to better understand potential distributional impacts before policies are implemented, monitor the implementation, and coordinate responses across government.

The report also provides practical and actionable solutions based on international experience that countries can implement to ensure that trade supports poverty reduction and shared prosperity. These include policies that reduce distortions and make it easier to do business, reduce trade costs through improved trade facilitation and logistics, and speed up labor market adjustment so that workers can find new jobs.

The gains from an open, rules-based international trading system can be seen every day. All countries stand to benefit when these gains are shared more widely and equitably.

Mari E. Pangestu
Managing Director, Development Policy and Partnerships
The World Bank Group

Acknowledgments

The preparation of this report was led by Gladys Lopez-Acevedo and Maryla Maliszewska. Core team members included Jakob Engel and Deeksha Kokas. The team is grateful to Laura Wallace for her skillful editing of the report.

Extended team members who prepared background papers and databases included the following colleagues: Erhan Artuç, Paulo Bastos, Diego Cardozo, Rakesh Gupta, Eunhee Lee (University of Maryland), Israel Osorio-Rodarte, Guido Porto (Universidad Nacional de La Plata), Bob Rijkers, Raymond Robertson (Texas A&M University), Carlos Rodríguez-Castelán, Nicolas Santos, and Hernan Winkler.

The team is very grateful to the peer reviewers for their excellent comments and suggestions: Paul Brenton, Maurizio Bussolo, and Andrew L. Dabalen. The work greatly benefited from guidance and encouragement by Benu Bidani, Caroline Freund, William Maloney, Ambar Narayan, Antonio Nucifora, and Carolina Sanchez-Paramo.

Useful comments were received through the preparation of the report from Ndiame Diop, Francisco H. G. Ferreira (London School of Economics), Daniel Lederman, and Pedro Olinto.

Administrative support came from Karem Edwards and Tanya Cubbins. The publishing team was skillfully led by Amy Lynn Grossman and Jewel McFadden. Alejandro Espinosa designed the cover. The communications campaign was run by Erik Churchill, Paul Gallagher, Elizabeth Howton, and Elizabeth Price.

About the Authors

Jakob Engel is an economist in the Macroeconomics, Trade, and Investment Global Practice at the World Bank. His expertise is in trade policy, political economy, regional integration, and commodity markets. He is the author of numerous research reports, journal articles, and chapters in edited volumes. Before joining the World Bank, he worked for the UK Department for International Development, the Overseas Development Institute, and the Smith School for Enterprise and Environment at the University of Oxford.

Deeksha Kokas is a consultant in the World Bank's Poverty and Equity Global Practice. Her current research covers trade, welfare, poverty, jobs, and digitization. She has been extensively researching the labor market adjustment process in response to globalization shocks. She has also worked on finance and private sector issues as part of the World Bank's Development Research Group and the Trade and Competitiveness Global Practice. Outside the World Bank, she has experience in conducting impact evaluations as part of J-PAL South Asia. She received a master's degree in economics from University College London.

Gladys Lopez-Acevedo is a lead economist and global lead at the World Bank in the Poverty and Equity Global Practice. She works in the South Asia and Middle East and North Africa regions. Her areas of analytical and operational interest include trade, welfare, gender, conflict, and jobs. Previously, she was a lead economist in the World Bank Office of the Chief Economist, South Asian Region, and a senior economist in the World Bank Central Vice Presidency for the Poverty Reduction and Economic Management unit working in the East Asia Region and in the Africa Region. She also worked in the Latin America Region at the World Bank. She is a research fellow at the Institute for Labor Economics (IZA) and at the Mexican National Research System. Before joining the World Bank, she held high-level positions in the government of Mexico and taught as a professor at the Instituto Tecnológico Autónomo de México (ITAM). She holds a BA in economics from ITAM and a PhD in economics from the University of Virginia.

Maryla Maliszewska is a senior economist in the Macroeconomics, Trade, and Investment Global Practice at the World Bank. Her area of expertise covers various aspects of trade policy and regional integration with a special focus on the impacts of trade on poverty and income distribution. She specializes in global analyses of structural and demographic change, as well as trade policy, using computable general equilibrium models. She contributed analyses underlying several World Bank reports and publications: *China 2030, Global Monitoring Report, Global Development Horizons,* and *Global Economic Prospects.* She joined the World Bank in 2010. Previously, she was a research fellow at the Center for Social and Economic Research in Warsaw, where she led several free trade agreement feasibility studies for the European Commission's Directorate General for Trade and conducted research on European Union trade policy, nontariff barriers, and modeling of trade flows, and was an adviser to the National Bank of Romania forecasting trade flows. She holds a PhD from the University of Sussex in Brighton, UK, and a master's in economics from Sussex, UK, and Warsaw University, Poland.

Abbreviations

ADH	Autor, Dorn, and Hanson
AfCFTA	African Continental Free Trade Area
CGE	computable general equilibrium
CGE-GIDD	Computable General Equilibrium–Global Income Distribution Dynamics
COVID-19	coronavirus
CPTPP	Comprehensive and Progressive Agreement for Trans-Pacific Partnership
FAMEX	Tunisian export-matching grant program
FDI	foreign direct investment
FTA	free trade agreement
GATT	General Agreement on Tariffs and Trade
GDLD	Gender Disaggregated Labor Database
GDP	gross domestic product
GIDD	Global Income Distribution Dynamics
GVC	global value chain
HIES	Household Income Expenditure Survey
HIT	Household Impacts of Tariff
H-O	Heckscher-Ohlin
ICT	information and communication technology
IT	information technology
MERCOSUR	Southern Common Market
NAFTA	North American Free Trade Agreement
PPP	purchasing power parity
PROCAMPO	Mexican program for direct assistance in agriculture
RCEP	Regional Comprehensive Economic Partnership
S-S	Stolper-Samuelson
TAA	trade adjustment assistance
TRAINS	Trade Analysis Information System
UN	United Nations
WTO	World Trade Organization

Executive Summary

The rise of international trade has transformed the global economy and coincided with a dramatic reduction in global poverty. From 1990 to 2017, global poverty fell from 36 to 9 percent, while developing countries increased their share in global exports from 16 to 30 percent. Many countries, especially those in East Asia, have used trade to create jobs, integrate into global and regional value chains, and reduce poverty. These countries built the infrastructure to support trade, reformed their economic policies to promote trade, and steered their youth toward jobs in industries that depended on trade.

Gains from trade do not accrue equally across and within countries, though, and some countries have struggled to mitigate the losses and make the gains from trade inclusive. Most countries have reduced tariffs, but nontariff barriers, poor infrastructure, and other impediments to trade continue to be prevalent across developing countries, raising trade costs and making it difficult to spread the benefits of trade. These impacts increasingly serve as an argument for protectionism and greater economic nationalism. The case against trade has increased in countries that have been unable to attract better export-oriented jobs or that offer little help for workers who experience trade-related dislocation.

The ways in which an abrupt rise or drop in trade—a trade shock—affects consumption and local labor markets, especially in developing countries, are complex and country-specific. As a result, trade policy makers in developing countries have found it difficult to predict how changes in trade policy might affect local labor markets and consumer prices.

To enable global trade to deliver for the poor, this report makes three primary contributions.

- It advances our understanding of how trade shocks affect consumers and workers, especially in developing countries, through new data, tools, and country analyses.

- It generates new findings through case studies on how trade has affected the poor as consumers and workers, depending on the type and duration of trade shock, labor market characteristics, transmission channels, location, and policy environment.

■ It provides a comprehensive set of complementary policies and economy-wide approaches to implementation that are necessary for trade to reduce poverty and inequality.

This report advances the policy maker's ability to analyze trade policy retrospectively, and it provides new methods for short- and long-term analysis of the impact of prospective trade shocks on communities and countries. The Household Impacts of Tariff (HIT) approach incorporates detailed consumption patterns at the household level and estimates short-term impacts of tariff line changes on consumption in low-income countries. The extension of the Global Income Distribution Dynamics (GIDD) approach provides greater granularity in the analysis of future trade policy changes, so that policy makers can assess the impact of reductions of tariffs, changes to nontariff measures, and improvements in trade facilitation at the subnational level. Reduced-form and structural approaches using detailed country-specific micro data allow for the study of impacts on local labor markets across time, regions, and demographic characteristics. Through a combination of methodologies, we can assess the impact of trade on a much larger set of outcomes affecting welfare, including income and wages, levels of formal and informal sector employment, consumption, poverty, and inequality at both national and subnational levels. Analysis conducted using these different approaches could help policy makers understand how to craft a reform agenda that distributes the gains from trade more widely.

This report provides new evidence that trade brings overall gains to households and is critical for lowering poverty, but it also shows that labor market and consumption gains tend to concentrate in some regions and worker categories. The persistence of these concentrated impacts has until recently been underappreciated and varies considerably across countries, suggesting that individual country studies are necessary. Impacts also differ over time, depending on the speed of the adjustment process. The informal economy in some emerging economies serves as a buffer, expanding after a trade shock to help workers adjust to changes in the labor market. Benefits such as lower consumer prices do not fully pass through to consumers, though, largely because of barriers related to geography, the market power of intermediaries, and the structure of domestic markets.

The report further deepens our knowledge about localized effects of trade through five empirical country studies. These describe (a) the impacts of apparel-led export growth on local labor market outcomes in Bangladesh, (b) labor mobility costs and their distributional consequences for welfare in Brazil, (c) the long-term effects of trade liberalization and their consequences on poverty in South Africa, (d) the impact of trade liberalization reforms on poverty and inequality in Mexican municipalities, and (e) the impact of trade policy reforms on employment at the subnational level in Sri Lanka.

Key findings from these case studies highlight very different political and economic dynamics that drive the differences in the impact of trade reforms on each country's economic outcomes and are invaluable from a policy perspective (table ES.1). Insights from these could inform policies to help mitigate losses and distribute gains from trade reforms more broadly. These studies also identify the population groups that may require additional support. Overall, they demonstrate that trade exerts substantial income and poverty effects that concentrate themselves in specific sectors and regions, differ over the long and short term, and can be both positive and negative. Beyond this, several key findings emerge.

- *Labor mobility and linkages between tradeable and nontradeable sectors are critical to spreading the gains from trade.* The studies on Brazil and Mexico look at the local distributional impacts of exports. In Mexico, higher manufacturing exports since the North American Free Trade Agreement show significant positive impacts on total labor incomes and employment in export sectors, but the impacts on poverty and local incomes are weaker. This could be driven by lower out-migration and higher inflows of return migrants from the United States, which has led to a disproportionate increase in unskilled workers at the municipality level who saw few gains from the positive export shock. In Brazil, lower export costs in the manufacturing sector affected workers in all sectors irrespective of their original sector. The manufacturing sector, though, primarily attracted workers from other industries within the same region because of large moving costs between regions and the relatively smaller economic benefits that accrued to workers in more remote regions.

- *Without compensatory public policies, trade liberalization can perpetuate historic disparities.* In South Africa, trade reform led to diversification and export growth, but certain historically underprivileged communities—those living in former homelands—experienced slower growth in employment and income per capita following trade liberalization reforms in the early 1990s than those living in the rest of the country. This seems to be driven by the historically low labor mobility across regions, sectors, and occupations that has characterized these territories. In Bangladesh, by contrast, a positive export shock caused only temporary regional differences in labor market outcomes, resulting in sustained wage gains and reductions in the gender wage gap.

- *Trade shocks can lead to higher rates of informal employment in the short term, but export gains generate incentives for these workers to reenter formal employment.* In Bangladesh, rising exports helped women transition into formal sector jobs. A US$100 gain in exports per worker between 2005 and 2010 led to a 0.7 percent decrease in informality in districts with a higher degree of exposure to trade. Similarly, an analysis of Brazil provides evidence that higher exports increased the number of workers in formal employment. Even in cases where informality increases, these jobs can serve as short-term buffers to support adjustment to trade shocks.

■ *New data and new techniques allow policy makers to design complementary policies to address subnational distributional impacts before a trade shock.* The forward-looking study on Sri Lanka focuses on the impact of potential trade policy reforms such as reductions in tariffs and nontariff measures, as well as the adoption of trade facilitation measures. It finds that lower trade barriers would speed up the expansion of gross domestic product and international trade and lower poverty but would also bring greater wage inequality. New analytical techniques also show that the impact of trade policy on employment varies at the subnational level. Without complementary policies, the gains would likely be concentrated in the most urbanized parts of the country. Efforts to improve the business environment and lower mobility costs could promote the spread of gains from trade to other regions beyond the existing urban centers.

A comprehensive set of complementary policies and economy-wide approaches is necessary for trade to promote poverty reduction and inequality. The report argues that policy choices made by governments can strongly influence the economic and political impacts of trade reforms, and it concludes by outlining a policy agenda that could foster inclusive trade outcomes. There are three types of complementary policies that could improve the distributional impacts of trade policy reforms: (a) reducing distortions and strengthening the functioning of markets, (b) reducing trade costs, and (c) speeding up labor market adjustment.

Beyond implementing the right complementary policies, there is a need to focus on the "nuts and bolts" of implementation at both the domestic and global levels. This includes a comprehensive and economy-wide approach that focuses on using new data and tools to understand potential distributional impacts before policies are implemented, monitoring the implementation, coordinating responses across government, and including extensive consultations with the private sector and other nongovernmental stakeholders.

In order to strengthen a global trade agenda that delivers benefits to the poor, it will be important to promote the multilateral trading system and increase its effectiveness in the context of rising protectionism. The COVID-19 (coronavirus) pandemic and the increasing frequency of climate-related shocks highlight the urgency for developing countries to strengthen the policy framework and economic foundations for resilient, competitive, and inclusive societies.

TABLE ES.1 **Case Studies Show Different Political and Economic Dynamics in Trade Reforms**

Case study	Knowledge gap study seeks to fill	Within-country results (labor income and consumption)	Distributional impact (differences across sectors, regions, types of workers)
Mexico		*Labor income:* Exports increase total labor incomes, that is, the sum of all labor incomes in the municipality. A 10 percent rise in exports per worker raises total labor incomes by 2.4 percent on average. However, since exports also increase labor supply at the local level, average labor incomes do not change. *Welfare:* Between 2004 and 2014, export growth led to higher income growth among households in the two poorest deciles in urban areas.	Since the positive impacts of exports on household incomes are concentrated in the poorest deciles, inequality falls. In particular, the Gini index declines by around 0.17 point (using a 0-100 scale) if the exports-to-worker ratio rises by 10 percent. Export growth increases in-migration and reduces out-migration at the municipal level, particularly of unskilled workers.
Bangladesh	Expansion of evidence on local distributional impacts of export shocks	*Labor income and informality:* Between 2005 and 2016, subdistricts more exposed to the export shocks experienced an increase in average annual wages in the short term (2005–10) relative to less exposed subdistricts and a decrease in informality in the short term (2005–10), with this spreading through the economy over time.	*Types of workers (wage income):* Average wage increases in subdistricts more exposed to the trade shock were substantially higher for men than for women, five times greater for high-skilled workers than for low-skilled workers, and twice as high for experienced workers than for younger workers. *Types of workers (informality):* Women seem to benefit more than men in terms of informality reduction related to trade effects, 1.5 percent versus 0.7 percent.
South Africa	Improved understanding of transitional dynamics of trade in local markets	*Labor income:* Between 1996 and 2011, a 10 percent reduction in employment-weighted tariffs led to a fall in income per capita of 1.4 percent outside the former homelands and a 3.7 percent reduction in income per capita in municipalities that included at least one former homeland.	Reduction in tariffs lead to those living in former homelands to experience slower growth in employment and income per capita than those living in the rest of the country.
Brazil	Development of a new tractable framework to quantify the impacts of trade shocks on labor mobility and the welfare of workers including the number of job opportunities	*Labor income:* Higher exports boost employment and wages. A 10 percent increase in exports leads to a 2.3 percent increase in employment and a 3.1 percent increase in average wages. Higher exports also increase the number of jobs on average and increase the number of workers in formal employment.	The magnitude of gains depends on a worker's industry as well as the region. The average increase in wages, for example, would be about 5 percent for manufacturing workers and more than 6 percent for manufacturing workers in regions with significant export concentration. The average real wage increase for agriculture workers would be about 3.75 percent, significantly smaller than that for most manufacturing workers.

(Table continues on the following page.)

TABLE ES.1 Case Studies Show Different Political and Economic Dynamics in Trade Reforms *(continued)*

Case study	Knowledge gap study seeks to fill	In-country results (labor income and consumption)	Distributional impact (differences across sectors, regions, types of workers)
Sri Lanka	Expansion of ex ante evidence on regional impacts on consumption and income in the medium to long term	*Welfare:* With lower trade barriers between Sri Lanka and its key trading partners, economic impacts would differ geographically as well as temporally. There would be less poverty but greater wage inequality and higher economic activity in urban areas than in rural areas.	Lower trade costs are likely to boost growth and output of sectors that employ a larger proportion of skilled workers (trade and transport, social services, and finance). As a result, wages of skilled workers grow faster than those of nonskilled workers, resulting (in the absence of policy intervention) in higher inequality. Most employment gains are projected in the western regions of Colombo, Gampaha, and Kalutara, where urbanization is highest.

1. Setting the Scene

Key Messages

- The rapid increase in global trade over the past 30 years has been a key engine of growth and poverty reduction in developing countries. From 1990 to 2017, global poverty fell from 36 to 9 percent at a time when developing countries increased their share of trade in gross domestic product from 34 to 48 percent.

- Although overall trade is still seen positively in many parts of the world, protectionist rhetoric and measures have been on the rise. This reflects concerns that gains from past reforms have often not been shared widely, impatience with the slow pace of adjustment after trade reforms in some countries, and, most recently, the global spread of the COVID-19 (coronavirus) pandemic, which is raising questions about reliance on foreign suppliers and the fragility of global value chains.

- To ensure continued support for trade, which will play a critical role in sustaining global economic activity during the pandemic, boosting economic recovery, and further reducing poverty, it is vital to clearly communicate how trade affects welfare across all segments of the population and its potential role in the reduction of global disparities, as well as the application of policies to ensure that gains are distributed more widely.

- This report fills gaps in the knowledge of how changes in trade affect within-country distribution—specifically between regions, industries, and demographic groups over time—through the labor market (wages and employment) and consumption channels, as well as across regions and time. With this knowledge, policy makers can craft better measures for maximizing gains from trade, ensure that the gains are more broadly distributed, and address adjustment costs more effectively.

Introduction

In the late 1980s and early 1990s, developing countries around the world liberalized their trade regimes, eliminating or drastically cutting high tariffs that were prevalent for most of the second half of the twentieth century. This opening up was driven by several factors: the widespread failure of import substitution policies; the collapse of the Soviet Union as an economic model competing with democratic capitalism; the export-led growth successes of economies like China and the Republic of Korea; and the reform agenda inherent to structural adjustment programs that many countries implemented in the context of escalating debt crises.

The globalization of supply chains, which benefited from declining transport costs and the spread of information and communication technologies, further increased the importance of trade and accelerated the fragmentation of global production across countries. Over this time period, the number of new bilateral and regional trade agreements also grew rapidly, and many existing ones expanded in scope. Global integration fundamentally reshaped industries and significantly realigned political dynamics within and between countries.

The opening up of economies went hand in hand with a much greater role for trade. From 1988 to 2019, trade as a share of gross domestic product (GDP) in developing countries increased from about 33 percent in 1988 to 49 percent in 2019 (figure 1.1), during which GDP growth in low- and middle-income countries was averaging 4.4 percent per annum. This shift also contributed to an unprecedented reduction in poverty: the global extreme poverty rate (under US$1.90 per day) declined from about 36 percent in 1990 to 9.2 percent in 2017 (the most recent available year), and the number of people in extreme poverty dropped from almost 2 billion to 689 million (figure 1.2).

Ever since the 2008 financial crisis, there have been worrisome signs about the future of trade and global integration. Growth in global trade, which recovered rapidly after the economic crisis, has slowed to a standstill since 2014. Additionally, opposition to many past trade deals and to new ones, especially in the West, has spurred a resurgence

FIGURE 1.1 As Tariffs Dropped in Developing Countries, the Role of Trade Increased

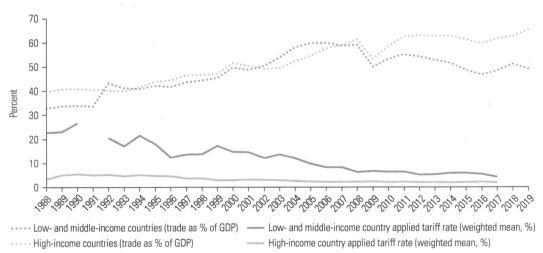

······ Low- and middle-income countries (trade as % of GDP) ——— Low- and middle-income country applied tariff rate (weighted mean, %)

······ High-income countries (trade as % of GDP) ——— High-income country applied tariff rate (weighted mean, %)

Source: World Development Indicators database (World Bank, various years).

Note: Data are unavailable for 1991 for the low- and middle-income country applied tariff rate.

FIGURE 1.2 Global Extreme Poverty Declined Sharply from 1990 to 2017

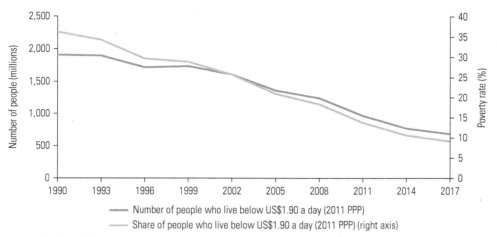

Source: World Bank 2020a.
Note: PPP = purchasing power parity.

in protectionist policies involving trade, investment, and migration since 2009 (figure 1.3). Such policies typically reflect concerns that gains from past reforms have often not been shared widely as well as impatience with the slow pace of adjustment after trade reforms. Although new trade agreements are still being negotiated, there has been a shift from multilateralism to regionalism. Examples include agreements such as the Regional Comprehensive Economic Partnership (RCEP) in East Asia, the Comprehensive and Progressive Agreement for Trans-Pacific Partnership (CPTPP), and the African Continental Free Trade Area (AfCFTA). The economic stress inflicted by the COVID-19 pandemic has magnified the existing concerns, raising questions about an over-reliance on foreign suppliers and the fragility of global value chains (see box 1.1).

This report comes at a time when a deeper understanding of the distributional impacts of trade is critical for the continued support for global integration and for the design of policies that allow the benefits of trade to be distributed more broadly. The shock from COVID-19 adds to an already uncertain trade policy environment in which trade relations between the United States and China have been deteriorating. Although several developing countries are pursuing either unilateral reforms, new free trade agreements like AfCFTA and CPTPP, or the expansion of existing free trade agreements, policy makers and companies are reassessing the viability of relying on global value chains, which now account for almost 50 percent of global trade (World Bank 2020b). The trade-off between resilience and efficiency could result in several companies increasing the geographical diversification of supply chains or even reshoring production (Freund 2020).

FIGURE 1.3 Restrictions on Trade, Investment, and Migration Have Increased in Recent Years

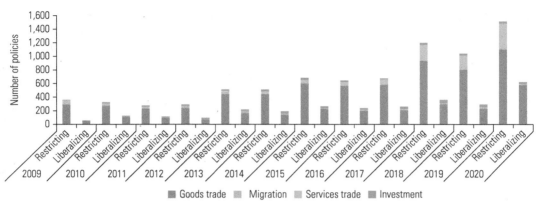

Source: Evenett and Fritz 2020.

BOX 1.1

The Spread of COVID-19 (Coronavirus) Poses a Significant Challenge to Global Integration

The global spread of COVID-19 (coronavirus) led many governments to respond by temporarily sealing borders and locking down economies, contributing to an unprecedented decline in global trade. Restrictions on movement to limit the spread of the disease shut down entire sectors of the economy, while the impacts of the pandemic have driven up trade costs and led to workers losing their jobs. Factories have been forced to close, and the cancellation of flights has affected freight capacity.

The recent collapse in demand has affected millions of workers in developing countries who had been able to escape poverty through jobs provided by export industries. Although some firms and industries are retooling to address the new demands of COVID-19—the Bangladeshi garment sector, for instance, is now producing masks and other medical goods required to address the pandemic—others have gone idle. Similarly, the new barriers to trade in food and other essential goods have created shortages and increased costs for the poorest.

Although there is still a great deal of uncertainty about the impacts of the pandemic, it is likely that it will delay progress toward achieving the Sustainable Development Goals by several years. A new World Bank analysis (Lakner et al. 2021) estimates that the impact of COVID-19 will likely push 119 million to 124 million into extreme poverty. As such, extreme poverty is projected to increase globally for the first time in three decades.

Maintaining trade flows during the pandemic will be crucial to providing access to essential food and medical supplies, as well as to limiting the negative impacts on jobs and poverty and sustaining global economic activity. Trade will also play a critical role in producing and distributing the vaccine at the global level and in facilitating an economic recovery by helping to strengthen the resilience of economies to future shocks (OECD 2020). Government efforts to encourage reshoring through subsidies for domestic sourcing could damage productivity and incomes, especially in developing countries where growth and poverty reduction were stimulated by their participation in global value chains (World Bank 2020b).

To ensure sustained support for trade, it is vital to clearly communicate how trade affects welfare across all segments of the population and its potential role in reducing global disparities. This report seeks to advance this effort by providing a deeper understanding of the within-country distributional impacts of trade—especially within regions, industries, and demographic groups—through the labor market and consumption channels. With that understanding, policy makers can craft more effective measures to maximize gains from trade, ensure that the gains are more broadly distributed, and better address adjustment costs.

Why Distributional Issues Matter

Changes in trade policy have distributional impacts that create winners and losers. Losses are often highly visible and concentrated, whereas gains are distributed more widely, undermining popular support in trade liberalization despite the aggregate gains (Artuç 2021; Artuç, Porto, and Rijkers 2019; Grossman and Helpman 1994). Two dynamics have come together to make this issue particularly salient now.

First, there have been substantial improvements in empirical methods, data collection, and computational capacity that have enabled the analysis of highly localized impacts over several decades. Recent studies show that the costs of moving across regions or industries can be far higher than previously assumed. In addition, the effects of trade on local labor markets can be large and long-lasting. Several high-profile books that draw on these studies (Banerjee and Duflo 2019; Rodrik 2017) also argue that insufficient attention has been paid to distributional impacts.

Second, there has been a growing awareness among policy makers in developing countries of differential impacts across industries, subnational regions, and population groups. So far, most of the work on the impact of trade on local labor markets has focused on trade shocks in developed countries, and it finds that the impacts of import competition are often localized and large.

Emerging evidence from developing countries shows mixed effects of trade on local labor markets. Some sectors have experienced significant losses due to greater import competition. Evidence from Brazil, for example, shows a painful adjustment for workers in import-competing industries after trade liberalization in the 1990s (Dix-Carneiro and Kovak 2017). There are other studies, though, showing that trade shocks have improved local labor market outcomes in South Asia and Vietnam. These findings from trade-related shocks on workers in select industries or regions have led to a growing body of research and analysis. This work is vital given that adverse distributional impacts associated with globalization increasingly serve as an argument for protectionism and greater economic nationalism, especially given the perceived lack of adequate policies to mitigate these losses. Currently, the global spread of COVID-19 is raising questions about many countries' dependence on foreign suppliers and the fragility of global value chains. Studies additionally show that inequality will worsen in nearly all economies in 2020–21 because the pandemic's economic impacts are disproportionately felt by people whose incomes are lowest (World Bank 2020a).

A good understanding of the distributional consequences of trade policies is key to achieving the World Bank's twin goals of reducing global extreme poverty and promoting shared prosperity by 2030. A recent study (World Bank 2018) finds that the only scenario whereby the Bank's target can be met and the global extreme poverty rate can be pushed below 3 percent by 2030 is one in which real growth rates are higher than in the past and income growth of the bottom 40 percent is 2 percentage points higher than the income growth of the top 60 percent. Trade can support faster economic growth, but understanding its impact on within-country inequalities over time will contribute to developing policies that address those inequalities and eradicate extreme poverty.

Value Added and Road Map

In recent years, the global community's understanding of the complex nature of the distributional effects of trade reforms and their policy implications, as well as the policies designed to mitigate adjustment costs and maximize benefits from integration, has improved substantially. There are still big knowledge gaps—notably the impact of trade changes on within-country distribution, especially across regions, industries, and demographic groups over time—that make it difficult for countries to make further progress. This report aims to fill some of those gaps and provide a foundation for better policy advice. It synthesizes two years of research, the development of new data sets and tools, and numerous other initiatives by World Bank teams, in consultation with outside experts. It also builds on and further develops a number of recent reports by international institutions that have addressed the links between trade reforms and welfare outcomes.

To analyze how trade affects distributional outcomes, the report takes advantage of the important changes in tariffs, access to intermediate inputs, and several notable trade shocks occurring in recent decades. Other mechanisms such as those unique to the rise of global value chains have been reviewed in depth by the World Development Report (World Bank 2020b). Furthermore, we only touch on the impact of nontariff barriers, trade in services, and improvements in trade facilitation and logistics that, while also affecting the relative prices of imports and exports, have particular effects worthy of future research. It is also worth noting that the report's focus is entirely on within-country distribution, leaving to future work a comprehensive analysis of the impacts of global trade on the global distribution of income.

This report's contribution falls into three key areas.

A snapshot of our knowledge to date and synthesis of key gaps. It provides a comprehensive review of the innovations in our understanding of the impact of trade policy changes on labor markets and consumer prices (chapter 2) as well as of the role of different complementary policy options to address these impacts (chapter 4). It highlights how the greater availability of microdata and advances in econometric and structural modeling techniques in the past decade have initiated a new wave of literature that measures the distributional impacts of trade within countries. One key insight is that geographically concentrated impacts can persist because of steep adjustment costs—a reality that can affect vulnerable groups even more severely—and that the magnitude of such costs has been previously underappreciated in the literature.

Country case studies to tackle knowledge gaps. This report tries to fill some of the knowledge gaps by examining how trade reforms have affected five low- and middle-income countries (chapter 3). It focuses on five empirical country studies of (a) the impacts of apparel-led export growth on labor market outcomes in Bangladesh, (b) mobility costs (sectoral, spatial, and occupational) and their distributional consequences on welfare in Brazil, (c) the long-term effects of trade liberalization on regional dynamics and their consequences for poverty in South Africa, (d) how trade liberalization reforms affected poverty in Mexican municipalities, and (e) the impact of trade policy reforms on employment at the subnational level in Sri Lanka. These countries offer a diversity of geographic contexts and development levels. They have undergone major trade reforms in recent decades, bear signs of geographic concentration and sluggish labor mobility, and offer high-quality data for the econometric analysis of local labor markets. Overall, the studies show that there are very different political and economic dynamics inherent in trade reform processes.

New methods and data sources. In the case studies, the report integrates a variety of methodologies such as backward- and forward-looking approaches, as well as partial and general equilibrium models, and applies the new tools to assess the distributional impacts of trade. These include (a) reduced-form and structural methods using detailed micro data to study impacts on local labor markets; (b) the extension of the

Computable General Equilibrium–Global Income Distribution Dynamics (CGE-GIDD) approach to local labor markets and (c) the Household Impact of Tariffs methodology, an online-based tool to simulate the first-order impacts of trade shocks on household income and consumption. The report furthermore provides new information and data sources, including a new global data set on wages, employment, and worker education at the two-digit sectoral level and the subnational (state) level based on data from the World Bank's Gender Disaggregated Labor Database.[1]

These new empirical studies that have produced several key findings.

- *Labor mobility and linkages between tradeable and nontradeable sectors are critical to equitably distributing the gains from trade.* The studies on Mexico and Brazil look at the local distributional impacts of exports. In Mexico, higher manufacturing exports since the North American Free Trade Agreement show significant positive impacts on total labor incomes and employment in export sectors, but the impacts on poverty and local incomes are weaker. This could be driven by lower out-migration and higher inflows of return migrants from the United States leading to a disproportionate increase in unskilled workers at the municipality level who were unable to reap the benefit of the positive export shock. In Brazil, lower export costs in the manufacturing sector affected workers in all sectors irrespective of their original sector. The manufacturing sector, though, primarily attracted workers from other industries within the same region because of large moving costs between regions. Consequently, workers in more remote regions benefited less.

- *Without complementary policies, trade liberalization can perpetuate historic disparities.* Despite trade reform leading to diversification and export growth, selected historically underprivileged communities in South Africa—those living in former homelands[2]—suffered slower growth of manufacturing employment employment following trade liberalization reforms in the early 1990s than those living in the rest of the country. This seems to be driven by low labor mobility across regions, sectors, and occupations. In Bangladesh, by contrast, regional differences in labor market outcomes after a positive export shock have been largely temporary, resulting in sustained wage gains and reductions in the gender wage gap.

- *Trade shocks can lead to higher rates of informal employment over the short term, but export gains generate incentives for workers to reenter formal employment.* In Bangladesh, rising exports helped many women transition into formal sector jobs. A US$100 gain in exports per worker between 2005 and 2010 led to a 0.7 percent decrease in informality in districts with a higher degree of exposure to trade. Similarly, higher exports increased the number of workers in formal employment in Brazil. Even in cases where informality increases, these jobs can serve as short-term buffers to support adjustments to trade shocks.

■ *New data and new techniques allow policy makers to design complementary policies to address subnational distributional impacts before a trade shock.* The forward-looking study on Sri Lanka focuses on the impact of potential trade policy reforms such as a reduction of tariffs and nontariff measures and the adoption of trade facilitation measures. It finds that lower trade barriers would lead to a faster expansion of GDP and international trade as well as lower poverty, but it would also produce greater wage inequality. New analytical techniques additionally show that the impact of trade policy on employment varies at the subnational level. Without complementary policies, the gains would likely be concentrated in the most urbanized parts of the country. Efforts to improve the business environment and lower mobility costs could promote the distribution of gains from trade to other regions beyond the existing urban centers.

The report structure follows the schematic shown in figure 1.4. It begins with a review of the literature on distributional impacts (chapter 2), then provides an overview of five developing country case studies that were prepared for this project (chapter 3), and concludes with a policy agenda to improve distributional outcomes from trade (chapter 4).

Understanding distributional impacts. Chapter 2 reviews the new wave of empirical and theoretical work covering the impacts of trade at the local or subnational level. It does this by examining the impact of trade on household welfare, focusing on the labor market and consumption channels. It concentrates on studies between 2000 and 2020 that are methodologically rigorous, have measured causal impacts, and focus on developing countries. The chapter suggests that there is clear evidence that trade brings overall gains to households, which is critical for lowering poverty. Labor market and consumption gains nonetheless tend to be concentrated in some regions and groups, and these concentrated impacts persist owing to steep adjustment costs.

FIGURE 1.4   Structure of This Report

Source: World Bank.

New empirical studies on country reforms. Chapter 3 provides an overview of five country case studies of low- and middle-income countries—Mexico, Bangladesh, South Africa, Brazil, and Sri Lanka—to shed more light on knowledge gaps and test some of the empirical lessons from earlier studies. The chapter demonstrates the varied political and economic dynamics inherent to trade reforms. Taking these dynamics into account can help governments shape better policies to support those losing out and more broadly distribute the benefits.

A policy agenda to foster inclusive trade outcomes. Chapter 4 explains how different types of complementary policies help support broad-based gains from trade reforms, especially in developing countries, and alleviate some of the potential adverse consequences. Three types of complementary policies can improve the distributional impacts of trade policy reforms: reduce distortions and strengthen the functioning of markets, reduce trade costs, and speed up labor market adjustment. The chapter concludes with a focus on the "nuts and bolts" of implementing policy that delivers for the poor at the domestic and global levels.

In sum, it is more important than ever that we better understand the distributional implications of trade, both within and across countries, and not just focus on the implications for a country in aggregate. These dynamics are often overlooked or poorly understood, and make it difficult for policy makers to ensure broad-based gains from trade. This report takes up the challenge, building upon innovative tools and methodologies to fill in some of those gaps.

Notes

1. See http://datatopics.worldbank.org/gdld/.
2. This refers to the 10 territories established by the apartheid government to concentrate members of discriminated ethnic groups.

References

Artuç, Erhan. 2021. "Distributional Effects of International Trade: Misconceptions about Losses and Gains." Research and Policy Brief, 44, World Bank, Washington, DC.

Artuç, Erhan, Guido Porto, and Bob Rijkers. 2019. "Trading Off the Income Gains and the Inequality Costs of Trade Policy." Policy Research Working Paper 8825, World Bank, Washington, DC.

Banerjee, Abhijit V., and Esther Duflo. 2019. *Good Economics for Hard Times: Better Answers to Our Biggest Problems*. London: Penguin UK.

Dix-Carneiro, Rafael, and Brian K. Kovak. 2017. "Trade Liberalization and Regional Dynamics." *American Economic Review* 107 (10): 2908–46.

Evenett, Simon J., and Johannes Fritz. 2020. *The GTA Handbook*. July 14, 2020. https://www.globaltradealert.org/data_extraction.

Freund, Caroline. 2020. "Governments Could Bring Supply Chains Home. It Would Defy Economic Rationality." *Barrons*, May 1, 2020. https://www.barrons.com/articles/will-supply-chains-come-home-after-the-coronavirus-recession-51588327200.

Grossman, Gene M., and Elhanan Helpman. 1994. "Protection for Sale." *American Economic Review* 84 (4): 833–50.

Lakner, Christoph, R. Andres Castenada Aguilar, Daniel G. Mahler, Haoyu Wu, and Nishant Yonzan. 2021. "Updated Estimates of the Impact of COVID-19 on Global Poverty: Looking Back at 2020 and the Outlook for 2021." *World Bank Data Blog* (blog), January 11, 2021. https://blogs .worldbank.org/opendata/updated-estimates-impact-covid-19-global-poverty-looking-back -2020-and-outlook-2021.

OECD (Organisation for Economic Co-operation and Development). 2020. "COVID-19 and International Trade: Issues and Actions; OECD Policy Responses to Coronavirus (COVID-19)." Working paper, OECD, Paris. http://www.oecd.org/coronavirus/policy-responses/covid-19-and -international-trade-issues-and-actions-494da2fa/.

Rodrik, Dani. 2017. *Straight Talk on Trade: Ideas for a Sane World Economy.* Princeton, NJ: Princeton University Press.

World Bank. 2018. *Poverty and Shared Prosperity 2018: Piecing Together the Poverty Puzzle.* Washington, DC: World Bank.

World Bank. 2020a. *Poverty and Shared Prosperity 2020: Reversals of Fortune.* Washington, DC: World Bank.

World Bank. 2020b. *World Development Report 2020: Trading for Development in the Age of Global Value Chains.* Washington, DC: World Bank.

2. Lessons from the Literature on Distributional Impacts

Key Messages

- There is clear evidence that trade brings overall gains to households and is critical for lowering poverty. Labor market and consumption gains, however, tend to concentrate in some regions and among some groups.

- These concentrated impacts could persist because of steep adjustment costs (more so for vulnerable groups), the magnitude of which was previously underappreciated. They are related to geographical barriers, policy distortions, and industry- and occupation-specific human capital.

- Subnational labor income and the employment effects of trade are large and can be negative or positive depending on the type of trade shock. They also differ over time depending on the speed of the adjustment process.

- Trade liberalization can produce benefits for the poor through lower consumer prices but these are often not fully passed on to consumers because of barriers related to geography, the market power of intermediaries, and the structure of domestic markets.

- Key gaps remain in our understanding of how trade shocks affect consumption and local labor markets, especially in low-income countries, as well as transitional dynamics from the short to long term. Despite advances in recent decades, the local impact of higher exports (as opposed to the impact of import competition and lower tariffs) has remained understudied. Other areas identified for further work include the role of informal labor markets as an adjustment mechanism in developing countries and distributional impacts propagated through global value chains.

Introduction

Compelling empirical evidence regarding the ways in which trade affects income distributions within a country has emerged in the past two decades.[1] The scope of analysis has consequently widened to examine broader dimensions of worker exposure to trade shocks, which underscore the complexity of the links between trade, inequality, and poverty. Previous surveys of the literature suggest that this complexity occurs for at least three reasons.

First, defining and measuring trade and its impacts are complex. Although the general idea of "trade" is straightforward, the variables used to measure trade vary. As such, it is perhaps not surprising that the empirical results in the literature often generate conflicting results. "Trade" variables include trade policy changes, value chains, output prices, outsourcing, and exchange rates. Much but not all of the current literature focuses on import competition or falling tariffs, leaving other dimensions understudied (Milanovic and Squire 2007; Rojas-Vallejos and Turnovsky 2017; Wood 1997).

Changes in trade may affect the economy either through prices (producer or consumer prices) or quantities (the volume of exports or imports). Although most approaches suggest that prices are the most relevant channels, many studies focus on quantities because they are usually easier to measure. Trade also affects consumer prices and not just wages. However, most studies approximate the impact of trade on welfare by examining how much wages can buy, using the changing price of a fixed basket of goods as a reference point. This may not account for differences in baskets consumed by poor and rich which have distributional implications (Ortiz-Ospina and Beltekian 2018). Studies measuring the distribution of welfare gains across all the main relevant welfare channels are only beginning to emerge.

Second, the range of labor market outcomes affected by trade shocks is broad. Employment, earnings, income inequality, informality, and unemployment are all critical dimensions that deserve attention. Earnings are most often studied, but other dimensions represent important aspects of worker welfare and opportunity. Informality, for example, plays a key role in developing country employment. When workers do not have income support such as unemployment insurance or government income assistance, working is necessary for survival. As a result, informal work is common and plays the role that unemployment insurance might play in developed countries.

Third, a greater appreciation of the differences between short-term adjustment and long-term effects is essential. Much of the current conventional wisdom about the rise in inequality resulting from trade shocks focuses on the short term, which is defined as the period in which workers and capital do not shift between industries. As labor and capital become more mobile, they incur significant adjustment costs. New insights into the importance and role of these adjustment costs raise the possibility that localized costs of international trade are higher than previously believed, possibly helping to explain why support for protectionism and tariffs have been rising in some countries. In the long term, however, the benefits tend to emerge in terms of decreasing wage inequality[2] (Beyer, Rojas, and Vergara 1999; Gonzaga, Filho, and Terra 2006; Robertson 2004).

A Framework for Understanding the Distributional Impacts of Trade

There are a few existing frameworks in the literature that provide a good starting point for understanding the varied channels through which trade can affect household welfare. Deaton (1989), for example, provides a simple framework that shows how households can be affected by price changes through both consumption and earnings after the removal of an export tax. Porto (2006) expands on Deaton's framework by distinguishing between the direct and indirect impacts of such trade policy changes between tradable sectors such as agriculture, manufacturing, and mining, and nontradable sectors such as infrastructure and retail. McCulloch, Winters, and Cirera (2001) provide a framework that traces the changes in border prices as a result of trade policy shocks to (a) retail prices faced by consumers; (b) impacts on firm profits, wages, and employment; and (c) effects on government revenue and expenditures on behalf of the poor. Drawing upon these frameworks, this report presents a simple guidance framework to systematically think about distributional impacts of trade.

First, households can be seen as both producers and nonproducers that consume as well as participate in the labor market. An advantage of separating the components in the definition of household welfare allows us to study producers and consumers independently in order to identify and quantify the different sources of welfare effects across households (Ural Marchand 2017).

Second, there are two key sources through which trade can affect welfare: prices and quantities. Among these, the following channels exist.

- *Prices.* One channel works via the impact on household expenditure. Changes in tariffs or other trade costs result in changes in border prices, wholesale prices, and eventually in retail prices, which alter the total cost of consumption for households. The consumption channel works via the impact on earnings. Changes in wholesale and retail prices result in changes to endowment prices, which affect firms' profits and thus lead to changes in investment and wage decisions. Wages obtained by households and profits earned by capital owners can increase or decrease as a result of trade policy shocks. Households could also see their income affected by the changing prices of items they produce.

- *Quantities.* Given that neoclassical trade models assume full employment and no barriers to labor mobility, they do not predict large effects of trade policy on employment levels. As firms' competitiveness changes because of shifts in the prices of inputs (imported and domestic) and outputs, both wage and employment decisions could be altered at the sector level. The ability of households to maintain or gain new employment might consequently be affected.

Third, there are differences in initial endowments or assets. The magnitude of the impact for different households depends on the markets and services they use—for example how much they consume of each product and which industry employs household members. This in turn is influenced by a household's endowments: skill levels, the ability to learn new skills, location, the ability to move, and its position in the income distribution.

Fourth, trade policy changes alter government revenue. The direct effect of the reduction of tariffs (or other trade taxes) might lead to lower tariff revenue; however, if it stimulates more demand for imports or increases economic activity and revenue from other taxes, the overall impact on government revenue could be positive. Changes in tax revenue could alter the value of government expenditures on behalf of the poor, including direct transfers to households.

Overall, trade policy shocks can have varied impacts on households with different income levels and other characteristics and can result in an overall pro-poor, pro-rich, or neutral effect. In the next section, we use this guidance framework to review the evidence documenting the impact of trade on household welfare with a focus on the labor market and consumption channels and across regions and time. We concentrate on the impacts on labor market and consumption outcomes because two-thirds to three-quarters of national income accrues to wage earners in developing countries, and labor continues to be the main asset for the poor. Also, a vast majority of households in low-income countries are self-employed and may not participate in the labor market (Goldberg and Pavcnik 2007a). In addition, we discuss how impacts vary across different groups on the basis of the demographic characteristics of workers and the income distribution.

This chapter draws upon Kokas and Engel (forthcoming), which provides a detailed review of the literature on distributional impacts of trade in developed and developing countries over the last three decades. It also draws upon other World Bank publications that discuss the distributional impacts of trade in detail (such as Artuç et al. 2019). In this chapter, we concentrate on studies between 2000 and 2020 (and especially the more recent ones) that are methodologically rigorous, have measured causal impacts, and focus on developing countries, while drawing on comparisons to developed countries. The coverage of studies is exhaustive in terms of methodologies being employed, and they include (a) partial equilibrium or reduced-form studies using quasi-experimental variation in cross-regional exposure to trade shocks (such as Dix-Carneiro and Kovak 2015, 2017; Edmons, Pavcnik, and Topalova 2007; Hasan et al. 2012; Kovak 2010; Topalova 2010); (b) studies that analyze regional impacts of trade in general equilibrium settings[3] (such as Caliendo, Dvorkin, and Parro 2019; Goés et al. 2019; Monte 2015); (c) studies that analyze labor market adjustment costs associated with trade shocks (using structural models such as Artuç, Chaudhuri, and McLaren 2010; Cosar 2013; Kambourov 2009; or using observational data such as Dix-Carneiro and Kovak 2017); and (d) studies that capture impacts on consumer prices, using household expenditure data or quantitative models with an emphasis on commodity markets and their role in determining welfare impacts (such as Faber 2014; Fajgelbaum and Khandelwal 2016; Porto 2006).

Impacts on Labor Market Outcomes

Over the past decade, a new wave of literature has surfaced that captures the impacts of trade at the local or subnational level and by region of residence of workers. It argues that the impacts of trade on local labor markets within a country may differ because of differences in their initial sectoral composition. Following Mexico's joining of the North American Free Trade Agreement (NAFTA), for example, workers in northern Mexico, which was more export-intensive, benefited more than workers living in regions far from the United States. This new wave of literature also builds on a vast evidence base describing trade impacts on labor markets within countries that has evolved over the past decades in terms of how it views workers, shifting from a focus on physical or human capital to industry affiliation, worker age, and the type of tasks being performed.[4] As highlighted by Robertson (2018), the differential impacts across regions occur primarily for two reasons.

- *Geographical concentration of production.* Production tends to be geographically concentrated or localized, and when this occurs lower-cost imports of a good will benefit consumers of that good nationwide. Areas with a high concentration of producers competing with these imports, by contrast, will experience a fall in employment. Similarly, areas with a high concentration of export-oriented producers will benefit.

- *Sluggish mobility across regions.* Faced with high moving costs, workers avoid moving between regions, and, if relocation costs are significant, trade liberalization effects will be highly localized.

A good place to begin is with a review of this literature that examines the welfare impacts of trade through the new lens of regional variation within developed and developing countries. The seminal study is by Topalova (2010), who focuses on the impact of India's trade liberalization. Since then, the academic community has analyzed the impacts of trade on labor market outcomes at the subnational level in developed countries, specifically focusing on the period leading up to and following China's accession to the World Trade Organization in 2001. This analysis includes China's rapid subsequent expansion in exports of low-skill-intensive manufactured goods to the United States and other industrial nations.

The most influential paper is by Autor, Dorn, and Hanson (2013, henceforth ADH), who analyze the effect of rising Chinese import competition between 1990 and 2007 on US local labor markets, examining cross-market variations in import exposure stemming from initial differences in industry specialization and instrumenting for US imports. The authors find that China's rise accounts for about 25 percent of the decline in US manufacturing employment, producing highly differentiated local impacts. The authors find that there was surprisingly no statistically significant impact on manufacturing wages, but there was a decline in wages outside of the manufacturing sector.

Turning from the local labor market as the unit of analysis to individual workers within local labor markets, Autor et al. (2014) find a differential wage impact of the China shock across local labor markets: Chinese import competition depressed wages, but high-income workers were affected less adversely than low-income earners. This contrasts with ADH, who find no effects on wages. Overall, the evidence to date on wage effects from the China shock does not appear strong.

Another important study comes to a similar conclusion. Pierce and Schott (2016), who focus on the same channel (direct competition from China), find that imports from China lowered US manufacturing jobs and total employment. Other reduced-form studies (following the same methodological framework as ADH) and other general equilibrium spatial model–based studies put estimates of US jobs lost due to trade with China at nearly 1 million (Caliendo and Parro 2015). Ten years after the rise of Chinese import competition, though, the areas adversely affected by trade had very similar populations: workers, in other words, did not want to relocate even after nearly a decade of import competition, highlighting severe labor adjustment costs. Several other studies focusing on the experience of developed countries with greater import competition find similar negative impacts on employment (Acemoglu et al. 2016; Asquith et al. 2017; Bernard et al. 2020).

ADH's contribution to the literature has been significant in terms of quantifying an inarguably exogenous shock—China's growth—and has stimulated an entire body of literature that assesses the impact of this shock on subnational labor market outcomes using reduced-form methodologies. Many of these papers have added more complexity to the ADH framework (see box 2.1). Xu, Ma, and Feenstra (2019), for instance, find that the negative employment effect of the China shock is reduced by about 20–30 percent when controlling for local housing prices. Another paper by Feenstra, Ma, and Xu (2017) contend that just focusing on Chinese exports is insufficient, given that the negative employment effects of Chinese imports on aggregate employment were offset by the positive effects of US exports.

Since the ADH study, empirical evidence has expanded to include emerging economies, although most studies have focused solely on estimating the downsides of increased import competition or falling tariffs on local labor markets (Dix-Carneiro and Kovak 2017; Kovak 2013). Some recent studies have quantified the gains in export-producing regions or industries, but only a handful have investigated

Extensions of "The China Syndrome"

With almost 3,000 citations since its publication in 2013 in the *American Economic Review*, "The China Syndrome: Local Labor Market Effects of Import Competition in the United States" by Autor, Dorn, and Hanson has exerted a seminal impact on analyzing the relationship between trade and employment. With this has come increased scrutiny of its findings, including its consideration of trade in intermediate inputs and the aggregate effects on welfare.

Trade in intermediate inputs. The China shock increased not only the exports of final goods from China to industrial nations but also those of intermediate goods. Extending the ADH framework, several papers use a similar reduced-form specification but use intermediate input imports rather than total imports in computing the trade exposure. An influential study is Wang et al. (2018) argues that the negative employment effects found by ADH are offset if benefits from Chinese imports that serve as inputs into other downstream sectors are considered. The authors find job losses from two channels: (a) the direct competition channel (for example, US firms that directly compete with Chinese imports) and (b) the upstream channel (for example, US firms that sell their outputs to other firms affected by Chinese imports). But these negative impacts are more than offset by benefits accrued from downstream US firms that use Chinese imports as inputs. Once the authors account for all three channels of exposure to trading with China, they find a positive boost to local employment and real wages.

Aggregate effects on welfare. The other key refinement of the ADH approach has been to extend this cross-regional reduced-form specification to capture aggregate economy-wide effects by incorporating information on interregional linkages. Accordingly, a recent body of literature has surfaced that not only studies the regional impacts of Chinese imports but also discusses the effects beyond the labor markets. It uses general equilibrium spatial models that allow for intermarket linkages, facilitating an analysis of how trade shocks affect aggregate welfare. Some of the key studies using these more comprehensive models find positive net economic effects of China's growth (Adão, Arkolakis, and Esposito 2019; Caliendo, Dvorkin, and Parro 2019; Galle, Rodríguez-Clare, and Yi 2017).

the longer-term effects of exports on labor market outcomes (Artuç et al. 2019; McCaig and Pavcnik 2018).

Although the channels of impacts are country-specific, some key messages can be drawn from the new body of literature that captures the impacts of trade at the local and subnational levels and by region of residence of workers.

First, effects of trade on labor income and poverty are large, localized (geographically concentrated), and limited to certain sectors and occupations. These could be negative or positive, depending on the type of trade shock faced by a country. When workers live in areas characterized by an industry losing its previous protection from import competition, they can experience significant welfare losses. Evidence from European countries and the United States support this finding. Global value chain participation through backward and forward linkages, though, seems to reduce poverty at the subnational level. In Mexico and Vietnam, the regions that saw more intensive global value chain participation also saw a greater reduction in poverty (World Bank 2020). Similarly, studies that look at the impact of greater export orientation and access to developed country markets find that in India wages are higher and labor shifts away from informal to formal jobs (Artuç et al. 2019), and in China and Vietnam poverty is lower and labor shifts out of agriculture (Erten and Leight 2019; McCaig and Pavcnik 2018).

Second, subnational impacts differ in both the short run and the long run depending on the adjustment process. In some countries, local labor market adjustments to trade shocks can be remarkably slow, with outcomes like wages and employment remaining depressed for a long period of time in the areas subject to more import competition from China (Autor, Dorn, and Hanson 2016). In Brazil and South Africa, recent work also finds that wage and employment impacts in regions more exposed to import competition can be long lasting but that, in Bangladesh, regional differences dissipate, and women's wages rise in the long run relative to men's earnings after a rise in exports (see chapter 3).

Third, the informal sector could constitute an important margin of labor market adjustment to trade in developing economies. Moving into informal employment serves as a fallback for trade-displaced workers, preventing them from falling out of the labor force completely, especially in regions with more flexible labor regulations.

Fourth, differences in the types of imports being impacted by tariff reductions have differing effects on labor income. In Brazil, Menezes-Filho and Muendler (2011) find that low tariffs on intermediate inputs were associated with a lower likelihood of unemployment and higher formal sector employment. By contrast, Dix-Carneiro and Kovak (2017) find that lower tariffs had the opposite effect, resulting in higher informality in Brazilian microregions that were more exposed to tariff reductions, even 20 years after the trade reform. Similarly, after examining annual variations in tariffs between 1993 and 2001, Sarra and Bombarda (2018) find that regional exposure to Mexican tariff reductions boosted the probability of formal employment in tradable sectors, especially for men. The authors argue this to be driven by the fact that export-oriented sectors benefited from the fall in Mexican tariffs as intermediate inputs became cheaper.

Local Labor Markets in Developing Countries

South Asia: Greater Exports Produce Positive Impacts on Formality and Wages in India, and on Employment in Bangladesh

Earlier evidence on the subnational effects of trade has focused on India, although findings differ on how much increased import competition has affected regional labor markets.

- A study by Topalova (2007) finds that tariff liberalization during the 1990s led to a 2.0 percent increase in the poverty incidence and a 0.6 percent increase in depth of poverty in urban districts, representing a setback of approximately 15 percent in India's progress in poverty reduction during the 1990s.

- By contrast, Hasan, Mitra, and Ural (2007) find that the tariff reforms were not associated with higher poverty overall. In fact, the study shows that lower tariffs during the 1990s were associated with a 15 percent decline in urban poverty in states with flexible labor market institutions relative to other states. There was additionally no effect on rural poverty. Given that the authors use an estimation technique similar to Topalova (2007), they argue that the difference in results could be explained by their inclusion of measures for nontrade barriers.

- Topalova (2010) takes nontrade barrier measures into account, though, and still finds that poverty rose dramatically in both rural and urban India in the 1990s.

On the export side, however, the verdict is clear. Indeed, there is evidence that export growth has resulted in a large and persistent beneficial impact on formality and wages. Hasan et al. (2012) find that trade protection is negatively correlated with state-level unemployment, a correlation that is especially strong for states with high employment in exporting industries. They also find that lower tariffs reduce unemployment rates by about 41 percent in states with flexible labor markets and large export shares.

Using a reduced-form analysis, Artuç et al. (2019) find that, larger exports per worker have resulted in higher wages for those typically working in the formal sector (especially high-skilled workers) and less informality for many marginalized groups in India (1999–2011) and Sri Lanka (2002–13).

- In districts in India that are more export-intensive, a US$100 export increase per worker resulted in an annual wage increase of Rs 572 per worker. Higher exports also drew workers from the informal sector into the formal sector, especially women and low-skilled workers.

- For Sri Lanka, a US$100 increase in exports per worker resulted in an average wage increase of SL Rs 975 and an average income increase of SL Rs 206.

Besides the study by Artuc et al. (2019), little is known about how trade barriers affect local labor markets in Sri Lanka. This report consequently tries to fill a gap by assessing the impact of Sri Lanka's potential trade policy changes not only on household income (through wages and sector of employment) but also on consumption through sectoral price changes (see chapter 3). This is done with a computable general equilibrium (CGE) model linked to a microsimulation in a top-down approach, which is expanded to cover subnational regions. We also discuss economic implications of paratariff liberalization using both the CGE model and the Household Impacts of Tariffs (HIT) database and simulation tool (see box 2.2 for more details).

BOX 2.2

Understanding Winners and Losers with the Household Impacts of Tariffs Database

Trade reforms affect households in their role as microcommunities of consumers, producers, wage earners, and taxpayers. This means that the effects on a particular household depend on its income and consumption portfolios, which not surprisingly can vary greatly. Until recently, there has been a lack of readily available data to measure these impacts, information that is vital for identifying winners and losers and, in turn, informing policy reforms. But the Household Impacts of Tariffs (HIT) database can now shed light on this issue.

The HIT database is a publicly available household survey–based data set covering 54 developing countries. It was constructed by harmonizing representative household surveys with import tariff data from the United Nations Conference on Trade and Development. The sample comprises all low-income countries for which relevant nationally representative household survey data (that is, data with information on both household incomes and consumption spending) are available and a number of middle-income countries. It contains granular data for each percentile of the income distribution on the income derived from and consumption of 53 agricultural products. It also keeps track of spending on five different types of manufacturing goods and services, as well as transfers and wage income disaggregated by single-digit sector, 10 different types of nonfarm household enterprise sales, and various types of transfers.

Tariffs vary both across countries and across products. The average tariff across countries is 14.2 percent. Tariffs are highest on average in Bhutan (48.4 percent) and lowest in Iraq (5.0 percent), whereas countries with higher levels of gross domestic product per capita tend to have lower tariffs. As for products, the highest average tariff is 39.4 percent, but this masks considerable differences across countries: Sri Lanka levies a 125 percent tariff on cigarettes, and in Jordan the tariff on beer is 200 percent.

What would the HIT tell us about how agricultural trade reforms would affect welfare in developing countries? The HIT analysis first estimates the impact of a change in tariffs on prices and then assesses how much the resulting price changes affect consumption costs and incomes in different households. The sum of these impacts is how much a household's real income changes. These simulations measure only the first-order (short-term) impacts of tariff liberalization and do not capture second-order adjustments such as changes in the availability of products, changes in

(Box continues on the following page.)

Understanding Winners and Losers with the Household Impacts of Tariffs Database *(continued)*

consumption patterns, and productivity gains arising through increased availability of intermedi-ates, which may well dominate in the medium to long term. In addition, the analysis assumes perfect pass-through of changes in tariffs to prices, though different pass-through rates can in principle be accommodated by making adjustments to the selected tariff changes.

A paper using this database by Artuç, Porto, and Rijkers (2019) shows that a unilateral elimina-tion of agricultural tariffs would increase household incomes by an average of 2.5 percent. The costs of protectionism, though, vary greatly across and within countries: the average standard deviation of the gains from trade within a country would be 1.01 percent. Furthermore, agricultural tariff liberalization would be pro-rich in 29 countries in the sense that the top 20 percent richest households would gain proportionately more than the bottom 20 percent. The poor would nonethe-less benefit more than the rich in 25 countries. The authors also find that using disaggregated data is important, because using more aggregate data yields biased estimates of the average gains from trade.

Although their study has focused on tariff reduction, the HIT also has a much wider set of potential applications and can accommodate richer and more sophisticated modeling assumptions. Examples include assessing how European Union and US agricultural tariffs or regional trade agreements (such as the African Growth and Opportunity Act) affect house-holds in low-income countries, how food price shocks affect poverty and inequality, and how tariffs affect men and women. In the next chapter, we use the HIT database to simulate the implications for welfare of paratariff liberalization for Sri Lanka and contrast the results with the Computable General Equilibrium–Global Income Distribution Dynamics methodology. These results are also contrasted with findings from a reduced-form analysis using detailed micro data for Sri Lanka to study impacts on local labor markets (Artuç et al. 2019).

Unlike India, not many studies of Bangladesh have investigated how trade affects local labor markets. Bangladesh has been successful in accelerating its export growth over the years by mostly concentrating on the ready-made garments sector. In turn, its exports are far less diversified than those of its neighbors and other comparators. There is, though, a dearth of empirical evidence on how export growth driven by a few sectors has affected local economic outcomes throughout the country. A recent study finds that a greater export orientation triggers a short-term increase in both formal and informal employment, as well as a longer-run increase in self-employment (Goutam et al. 2017). Using a reduced-form model such as ADH, Goutam et al. (2017) find that trade increases labor force participation and formal employment in Bangladesh. Moreover, there is an even larger impact on labor force participation if the indirect impacts of trade in the form of induced demand through supply chain linkages are included. In this report, we expand this evidence by evaluating the impacts of greater export orientation in local labor market outcomes in Bangladesh, particularly wages and informality, for different demographic groups (see chapter 3). We also explore whether these trade shocks remain localized or if they spread throughout the economy.

Latin America: Painful Adjustment Process to Trade Liberalization in Brazil

For Brazilian workers, empirical evidence shows that the dynamic process of adjustment to trade liberalization reforms has been painful, bringing bigger declines in wages and lower employment over time.

Kovak (2013) finds that microregions in Brazil facing liberalization-induced price declines greater than 10 percent between 1991 and 2002 experienced 4 percent more declines in wages. Building upon this work, Dix-Carneiro and Kovak (2017) show that microregions facing larger tariff cuts experienced prolonged declines in formal sector employment and earnings relative to other microregions: the impact of tariff changes on regional earnings 20 years after liberalization is three times the effect after 10 years (figure 2.1). Workers initially working in tradable sectors are more likely to move to nontradable sectors, but this response is not enough to offset the strong declines in formal employment in tradable sectors (figure 2.2). Why does this occur? The authors suggest there is a mechanism involving imperfect interregional labor mobility and dynamics in labor demand, driven by slow capital adjustment and

FIGURE 2.1 Big Drops in Formal Employment Occur after Tariff Cuts
Average months of formal employment per year, tradable versus nontradable sectors

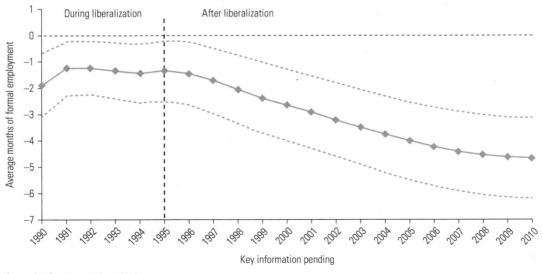

Source: Dix-Carneiro and Kovak 2017.

The Distributional Impacts of Trade

FIGURE 2.2 **Tradable Sectors Are Hardest Hit Even Decades Later**

Average months of formal employment per year, tradable versus nontradable sectors

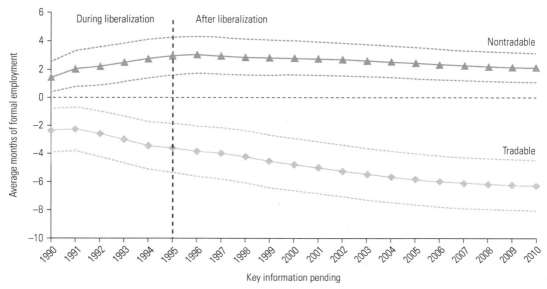

Source: Dix-Carneiro and Kovak 2017.

agglomeration economies. These unfavorable results are consistent with conclusions by Góes et al. (2019), who deviate from the reduced-form methodology employed by these earlier studies and instead use a general equilibrium model that aggregates information on production, employment, wages, prices, imports, and exports in 57 economic sectors in Brazil.

Most of the adjustment in Brazil takes place through the informal sector, which acts as a buffer for trade-displaced workers. Dix-Carneiro and Kovak (2017) show that, after Brazil's trade liberalization in the 1990s, microregions more exposed to foreign competition faced higher unemployment in the medium term relative to the national average. In the long run, however, foreign competition had no effect on unemployment, but there was a significant positive effect on informal employment at the local level. This view of the informal sector serving as a buffer is corroborated by Ponczek and Ulyssea (2018), who show that the medium-term effect of liberalization-induced foreign competition on unemployment was larger in microregions where labor market regulations were more strictly enforced, making labor shifts harder. The role of the informal sector as an important margin of labor market adjustment to trade has gained prominence in the literature in last two decades (see box 2.3).

Informal Labor Markets and Trade

A large share of the workforce (usually 40 to 80 percent) in emerging economies remains in informal labor arrangements (Arias et al. 2018); however, until recently, empirical and modeling work has neglected the study of informality.

There is now a greater appreciation that the informal sector could constitute an important margin of labor market adjustment to trade. One view argues that trade-related shocks may increase the size of the informal sector, whereas others suggest that the informal sector could serve as a buffer for trade-displaced workers in the medium term, preventing them from falling out of the labor force completely. This has led to a small but burgeoning literature examining the links between changes in trade and informal labor markets in the past two decades. Goldberg and Pavcnik (2007a) provide a review of earlier studies and find mixed impacts, depending on country and industry characteristics. Specifically, labor markets that are characterized by effective regulation tend to have more firms that favor informal employment (Artuç et al. 2019). But labor markets that are more flexible tend to have less informal employment after trade liberalization. This corresponds with work by Bosch, Goni, and Maloney (2012), which shows that the rise in informality in Brazil from 1983 to 2002 was driven to a much greater degree by rising labor costs and reduced flexibility than by trade liberalization.

More recent studies find similar patterns. McCaig and Pavcnik (2018), for example, find that the rise in exports in Vietnam driven by the United States–Vietnam Bilateral Trade Agreement led to a reallocation of labor from informal to formal manufacturing in the sectors most affected. By contrast, Dix-Carneiro and Kovak (2019) and Ponczek and Ulyssea (2018) suggest that the informal sector may serve as a buffer to trade-displaced workers and that, in the absence of informality, the effects of foreign competition on unemployment might have been more severe.

Most recently, a study by Dix-Carneiro et al. (2021) that applies a general equilibrium model of a small, open economy with labor market frictions and imperfectly enforced regulations to Brazilian data finds that repressing informality in the model increases productivity but at the expense of employment and welfare in the face of a trade shock.

What about the effects of an import and export shock on migration across microregions and labor reallocation from the formal sector to nonemployment within these regions? Using an instrumental-variable approach, Brummund and Connolly (2019) examine Brazil's unique trade relationship with China to analyze this question. They find that export exposure reduces the movement of workers from the traded sector to nonemployment and increases the movement of workers from nonemployment to the nontraded sector. These movements are primarily driven by the manufacturing sector. This is in stark contrast to the negative impacts on microregions that are more exposed to imports, which show more reallocation from manufacturing to nonemployment, and less movement from the traded sector to the nontraded sector. It thus seems that Brazilian labor markets responded more dynamically to the China shock than they did to the 1990s trade reforms.

Chapter 3 builds on this large body of evidence on Brazil and breaks new ground by deepening the understanding about what happens when there is a positive shock from higher exports. Specifically, we test the importance of labor friction costs along with job opportunities provided across regions and sectors. In doing so, our case study on Brazil bridges dynamic models of labor mobility and reduced-form differential exposure methods of quantifying the impacts of trade shocks on worker welfare.

East Asia: Reducing Poverty by Cutting Tariffs on Inputs in Indonesia and Increasing Exports in Vietnam

Unlike Brazil, Vietnam's experience of reallocation after trade reforms has been starkly different. In a study analyzing the labor market impacts of Vietnam's free trade agreement with the United States, McCaig and Pavcnik (2018) find a significant reallocation of labor from informal household businesses to employers in the formal sector. The reallocation was greater in industries and regions that experienced larger declines in US tariffs on Vietnamese exports and also among younger workers. The study also suggests that expanded export opportunities increased employment among manufacturing firms by 15 percent. At the same time, the aggregate share of household businesses declined in Vietnam during the early 2000s.

As for Indonesia, which has one of the highest mobility costs among developing countries, Agustina (2018) finds negative impacts of increased import competition between 2007 and 2013 on manufacturing employment share, nonmanufacturing employment share, and wages. And Cali, Hidayat, and Hollweg (2019) suggest that workers in more remote regions (especially in eastern Indonesia) face particularly high mobility costs. Not surprisingly, then, workers were unable to adjust to these trade shocks and became unemployed, with the highest impact driven by imports of consumption goods.

By contrast, the work of Kis-Katos and Sparrow (2015) and Kis-Katos, Pieters, and Sparrow (2018) shows positive labor market consequences across Indonesia's regions following the liberalization of trade in intermediate inputs. Specifically, the authors find that poverty decreased more in regions that were more strongly exposed to the liberalization of tariffs for intermediate inputs. In addition, job formation and increases in unskilled wages were related to lower import tariffs on intermediate goods with no changes in import tariffs on final outputs. This reiterates the point that it is vital to distinguish between the types of imports being affected by tariff reductions when analyzing the impacts of greater import competition on welfare.

Sub-Saharan Africa: Negative Impacts of Trade Liberalization on Employment Concentrated in Certain Regions and Groups

Not much is known about the local labor market impacts of trade in Sub-Saharan Africa, but a recent study on South Africa shows that trade impacts operate through the employment channel rather than the income channel. Erten, Leight, and Tregenna (2019) provide strong causal evidence on the effects of a quasi-exogenous reduction in import tariffs on local economies in South Africa between 1994 and 2004, the period of rapid trade liberalization. The results suggest that workers employed in districts facing larger tariff reductions experienced a slower growth in employment driven primarily by a decline in manufacturing sector employment relative to workers in districts facing smaller tariff reductions.

These displaced workers were unable to reallocate into other sectors. Instead, they were more likely to become discouraged, unemployed workers or exit the labor force entirely. Unlike in other countries, they also were not absorbed by the informal economy. When examining differences with respect to education and race, the observed employment effects were consistent for individuals at varying education levels, but among relatively less-educated workers, nonwhite workers faced a higher likelihood of employment loss. By contrast, there was no evidence of significant differences with respect to gender, age, or location. The study shows a concentration of negative impacts of trade on employment in certain regions or local labor markets and groups (black and other nonwhite workers), despite the reintegration of homelands into South Africa after 1994.

This report adds to this evidence base by further analyzing how persistent these impacts on local labor markets are in the medium to long term—given the sharp tariff reductions observed after the democratic elections—by drawing upon municipal-level data from South Africa for the period 1996–2011 (see chapter 3).

Understanding Hefty Adjustment Costs

The ability of workers to relocate between economic activities is an important factor in determining their resilience to trade shocks. Traditionally, neoclassical and other trade models have assumed adjustment to be costless or costs to be very small. Neoclassical trade theory assumes perfect, costless mobility among factors of production in which trade-induced price changes are assumed to have only economy-wide (not sector- or region-specific) returns. Other studies have deviated from this trend, contending that the long-run free trade equilibrium could be affected negatively by the existence of these adjustment costs. Davidson and Matusz (2004) show that the presence of inflexible labor markets can lead to multiple equilibria ("good" or "bad" steady states), given a trade policy change or shock. Banerjee and Newman (2004) develop a model in which the short-term costs of factor reallocation that follows trade liberalization fall disproportionately on the poor.

As for the limited number of empirical studies, they too conclude that adjustment costs are relatively small. Using the experience of developing and advanced countries during episodes of trade liberalization and structural adjustment, they categorically estimate that periods of unemployment are quite short and adjustment costs very small compared to the benefits of trade liberalization (Matusz and Tarr 1999, 2000; Papageorgiou, Choski, and Michaely 1990). Studies focusing on advanced countries find similar results, attributing large declines in manufacturing employment to technological innovation (Feenstra and Hanson 2001; Harrison, McLaren, and McMillan 2011). A feature of most of the earlier work on adjustment costs is the disproportionate focus on developed countries.

Over the past decade, there has been renewed inquiry into adjustment costs driven primarily by global economic changes (the growth of China, other East Asian countries, and Eastern European countries) and expanding empirical evidence. Several studies document the adjustment costs borne by workers after trade reforms in many developing countries (Pavcnik 2017; Revenga 1997; Currie and Harrison 1997). Moreover, studies focusing on the reallocation of workers across sectors find significant effects for developed countries (Pierce and Schott 2016; Revenga 1992), although they are less significant than in developing countries (Dix-Carneiro 2014; Goldberg and Pavcnik 2007a).

Artuç, Chaudhuri, and McLaren (2010) were among the first to attempt to estimate trade adjustment costs. They assume that migration decisions are based on the earnings possibility in a given destination (the option value). For the United States, they find very high average moving costs from one broadly aggregated sector of the economy to another. Specifically, worker-level adjustment costs are estimated to be as much as eight times annual earnings. They also predict a sluggish reallocation of workers following trade liberalization, with 95 percent of the process completed eight years after the elimination of a 30 percent tariff on manufacturing. Similarly high adjustment costs are found for Turkey, where wages in the formerly protected sector declined by as much as 20 percent (Artuç and McLaren 2010).

Over the past decade, labor market adjustment costs have become central in a new wave of trade models, and all these studies estimate very high adjustment costs (such as Adão 2016; Caliendo, Dvorkin, and Parro 2019; Dix-Carneiro 2014). Like Artuç, Chaudhuri, and McLaren (2010), Dix-Carneiro (2014) and Adão (2016) use a Roy model of the allocation of workers across sectors to offer a structural analysis of the distributional effects of trade shocks. Dix-Carneiro (2014) estimates a median cost of mobility that ranges from 1.4 to 2.7 times annual average wages in Brazil. Caliendo, Dvorkin, and Parro (2019) reiterate further the dynamics of adjustment after an unexpected trade shock. These models show that adjustment costs critically affect welfare. In extreme cases, high adjustment costs may overwhelm the positive benefits of trade liberalization.

Early papers treated these adjustment costs merely as a black box (as described by McLaren 2017), but more recent papers have been able to identify key components by studying labor markets in transition after a large trade shock. These adjustment costs fall into three key areas.

Geographical costs. Geography affects mobility costs, especially when industries are spatially concentrated. Some studies estimate that these moving costs are very high. One such study by Morten and Oliveira (2016) finds that migration generates heterogeneity in regional responses to trade shocks and also changes the incidence of regional shocks: 37 percent of the total incidence of a shock falls on residents, compared to 1 percent in a model where migration is costless. They also find that a region 10 percent more connected will have a 5.6 percent higher population elasticity to wage shocks.

Domestic regulations and policies. The speed of labor reallocation can be affected by the flexibility of labor markets: a flexible labor market will support the required reallocation of labor whereas a highly regulated labor market will slow it down. An important study in this regard is by Kambourov (2009), who use a dynamic general equilibrium sectoral model to analyze the inflexibility of labor regulations as a source of adjustment costs. He finds that, if Chile had not liberalized its labor market at the outset of its trade reform, then the intersectoral reallocation of workers would have been 30 percent slower, and as much as 30 percent of the gains in real output and labor productivity in the years following the trade reform would have been lost. Similar results were found for Mexico.

Gains from trade may not always be fully realized across regions because of certain existing domestic policies that could lead to institutional friction. Analyzing how the household registration system (*hukou*) affects migration and the extent to which it affects both aggregate and distributional effects of trade, Zi (2018) finds that China's *hukou* system, which prohibits migrant workers from accessing various social benefits in their actual cities of residence, leads to urban areas receiving smaller migration inflows following an increase in exports. She also finds that abolishing the *hukou* system increases gains from input tariff reductions by 2.0 percent and alleviates negative distributional consequences. Fan (2019) also shows that ignoring domestic geographic frictions leads to significantly underestimating trade's impact on overall inequality and overestimating its impact on the aggregate skill premium in China.

Sector- and occupation-specific human capital costs. Some studies focus on mobility issues that can arise from sector-specific worker experience or the nonadaptive nature of human capital. In analyzing an intersectoral reallocation of labor in response to trade reforms in Brazil, for instance, Cosar (2013) develops a small two-sector open economy model of equilibrium search with overlapping generations and sector-specific human capital. Simulation results show that labor market adjustment in response to a reallocation shock can take a long time because of a combination of labor market frictions and sector-specific human capital. The uniqueness of human capital at the sector level, though, poses a much bigger barrier to labor mobility than search frictions.

In contrast, using a dynamic equilibrium model with labor market frictions and occupation-specific human capital, Ritter (2012) finds that, in light of the surge in trade in goods and services observed between 1990 and 2010 in the United States, a flexible labor market plays a bigger role in the adjustment process than the specific human capital of workers in high-skill service occupations.

The bottom line is that large labor adjustment costs may lead to large unrealized gains from trade, and these costs could be triggered by geographical barriers, sector- or occupation-specific human capital barriers, or policy distortions. The understanding of these costs remains indispensable to better informing our knowledge of subnational impacts of trade, as well as understanding the different kinds of costs that workers bear. This is because governments will need to choose among a wide range of policies to help workers cope with job loss (see chapter 4).

This report focuses on labor market costs because they can be very high, can have considerable political influence, and are key in developing countries that are specialized in labor-intensive manufacturing. However, the nature of adjustment costs differs depending on the country context. In several low-income countries where the primary sector of employment, production, and trade is agriculture, for instance, adjustment at the smallholder or farmer level[5] is much more relevant than labor market adjustment costs. There are often also large capital adjustment costs in industrial production.

Impacts on Consumer Prices and Cost of Living

Viewing the distributional impacts of trade through the lens of household consumption is particularly relevant for low-income countries, given that a substantial share of the workforce are not formally employed. In these contexts, work often takes place in household businesses and family farms, and a substantial amount of time is devoted to producing goods and services used for personal consumption by the workers (Goldberg and Pavcnik 2007a). Impacts through prices or cost of living constitute a key piece in the discussion of distributional impacts of trade as individuals with different levels of income consume goods at different intensities, and the proportion of imported versus domestic goods significantly varies depending on the level of household income. Only a few publications explore this question, though, primarily because of data limitations. As previously highlighted by Goldberg and Pavcnik (2007a), household surveys so far have had a limited focus on the self-employed and a poor response rate to consumption questions.

Despite these challenges, the literature on consumption effects of trade integration has evolved in recent years, both in terms of methodological innovations and the aspects of globalization being studied (box 2.4). Whereas initial studies used reduced-form methods that relied on household consumption surveys and simulated price changes at the product group level (Deaton 1989; Porto 2006), more recent studies have used structural models with cross-country trade flows to quantify these impacts (Fajgelbaum and Khandelwal 2016). There has also been a growing interest in the shifts in purchasing patterns of households from traditional stores to foreign retailers, which

BOX 2.4

New Approaches to Measure Consumption Impacts

New methodologies. One innovation is the use of reduced-form and quantitative trade models to quantify the impact of trade integration on income inequality through its effects on the price index relevant to individuals with different income levels using the methodology outlined by Deaton (1989). The most heavily cited study is that of Porto (2006), who explores the impact of Argentina's trade reform on consumers by combining scheduled Argentine tariff changes under the Southern Common Market (MERCOSUR) with household expenditure shares across seven consumption sectors to simulate household inflation differences.

Since then, several studies have analyzed consumption and income channels to estimate the net effects of tariff reforms for developed and developing countries on welfare (Borusyak and Jaravel 2018; Hasan, Mitra, and Ural 2007; Nicita 2009; Nicita, Olarreaga, and Porto 2014; Ural Marchand 2012). Other studies have used quantitative trade models to estimate the impacts of changes in tariffs on consumption (Fajgelbaum and Khandelwal 2016).

New aspects of globalization. Shifting the focus away from changes in traditional measures of trade (like tariffs or export prices), a few recent studies have concentrated on other aspects of globalization (like retail trade and tariff reductions for intermediate inputs). Atkin et al. (2018) attempt to capture the first-order effects of retail globalization by using a rich collection of microdata to assess the consequences of expanding foreign direct investment in the retail sector in Mexico.

Faber (2014) examines Mexico's entry into the North American Free Trade Agreement to study the effect of input tariff reductions on the price changes of final goods of different quality. He shows that access to imported inputs reduces the relative price of higher-quality products in the country.

has led to retail trade as a source of potential benefits. Other studies have focused on how tariff reductions in intermediates affect consumer prices, given that a vast majority of developing country consumption has been increasingly driven by imported inputs rather than directly traded final consumer goods.

Whereas some studies just focus on estimating gains from trade through the consumption channel, others estimate the net welfare effect by studying both the consumption and income channels.

- *There are significant gains through the consumption channel and a pro-poor distributional effect across most countries.* Using a quantitative modeling framework, Fajgelbaum and Khandelwal (2016) analyze how international trade affects individuals through the expenditure channel for multiple countries. They find a pro-poor bias of trade in every country through the consumption channel. On average, the gains from opening to trade are 63 percent for the 10th percentile of the income distribution and 28 percent for the 90th percentile.

- *In many cases, though, these consumption gains are dwarfed by larger negative income effects, which lead to net welfare losses.* In Mexico, for example, net gains are regressive, with larger gains for richer households overpowering smaller gains for poor households (Nicita 2009).

- *Consumption effects are smaller for nontradable goods and bigger for urban and border areas.* The budget share of nontradable goods tends to be smaller among poor households, especially in developing countries. As a result, the direct effect of trade-induced price changes is more important for poor households, and impacts through nontradable goods remain smaller in several countries.

Delving deeper some recent studies highlight the gains from consumption and net gains from consumption and income and show that results vary across income distributions, regions, and different baskets of goods consumed by individuals.

India. Looking at just the consumption side, Fajgelbaum and Khandelwal (2016) find that opening up to trade in India is typically pro-poor, because the poor tend to consume a greater share of traded goods. The authors also show that moving from current trade shares to autarky would disproportionately hurt poor consumers more, but their approach does not address the supply side.

In another study, Ural Marchand (2012) addresses this gap by estimating the distribution of gains due to India's trade reforms by simultaneously considering the effect on prices of tradable goods and wages. Even after considering the demand and supply side simultaneously, he also finds the reforms to be pro-poor: an 18 percent welfare gain at the bottom end of the distribution versus 13 percent at the top end of the distribution between 1988 and 2000. These pro-poor gains are primarily driven by higher tariff reduction for commodities that are more important for poorer households and the higher share of unskilled labor among poorer households.

China. While assessing the impact of World Trade Organization accession on household welfare, Han et al. (2016) find welfare gains for almost every household across the per capita expenditure spectrum (at an average of about 7.3 percent). The distributional effect is strongly pro-poor: as high as 13 percent at the bottom end of the distribution but statistically insignificant at the top end. The authors also find that these net gains in welfare through nontradable goods and services are very small in magnitude, totaling only about 0.7 percent. They attribute this small economic benefit through nontradable goods to the small share of nontradable goods in consumption baskets across Chinese cities.

Argentina. Looking at both consumption and income effects, Porto (2006) finds that the regional Southern Common Market (MERCOSUR) trade agreement brought pro-poor net gains for Argentines. The poorest households experienced sizable gains versus a welfare loss for the richest households. These net gains were driven by pro-poor income effects, although consumption effects were found to be pro-rich. The study also finds the welfare effect through nontradable goods to be very small in Argentina, varying between 0.3 and 1.0 percent across the income distribution.

Mexico. Extending Porto's approach by adding a link from trade policy to domestic prices, Nicita (2009) studies the impact of Mexico's trade liberalization effects on the welfare of households. He finds that these reforms lower the domestic prices of several agricultural and manufacturing products and increase the wage gap between skilled and unskilled workers. Although all households gained from a cheaper consumption basket, households that were net suppliers of agricultural goods were hurt by the decline in income. Likewise, the downward pressure on unskilled wages hurt labor supplied by low-income households. Taken together, the net gains were regressive in Mexico, with larger gains for richer households overpowering smaller gains for poor households. There also were variations in these impacts across regions: states closer to trading markets, especially in the United States, benefited the most in terms of higher real income.

Sub-Saharan Africa. Incorporating three channels (production, skills, and consumption), Nicita, Olarreaga, and Porto (2014) find existing trade policies in six Sub Saharan African countries to be pro-poor. The key driver of this result is the protection of skilled labor, which predominantly benefits richer households, whereas the consumption channel is neither systematically pro-rich nor pro-poor.

United States. Similar effects can also be observed in the case of developed economies. In the United States, Borusyak and Jaravel (2018) find that the gains from trade are pro-poor on the expenditure side but are dwarfed by the effects on the earnings side. The negative impact of trade on earnings is significantly larger for less skilled workers, which more than offsets the gains on the consumption side.

Imperfect Pass-Through of Tariff Prices to Consumers

At the national level, as the literature demonstrates, most countries experience gains through the consumption channel, but there can be large variations within a country as to who benefits and by how much. Why does this occur? The answer centers on an imperfect pass-through of changes in tariff prices to consumers and to local labor markets.

In recent times, some of the literature has focused on analyzing the size of internal trade costs that separate consumers in remote locations of developing countries from global markets, and what those barriers imply for the domestic distribution of gains from falling international trade barriers. A review of this burgeoning literature highlights that the imperfect pass-through of tariff reductions to domestic prices may be driven by barriers related to geography, market power of intermediaries, and the structure of domestic markets.[6]

Geographical barriers. The pass-through of tariff reductions to domestic prices may be greater in areas closer to borders than in areas more distant, tempered by lack of competition in logistics. In Mexico, Nicita (2009) finds regional differences in tariff pass-through for manufacturing products. Tariff pass-through at the border is about 70 percent for manufacturing, declining to about 40 percent at 1,000 kilometers, and 20 percent at 2,000 kilometers from the border. Not surprisingly, limited pass-through is one explanation for the fact that real income has risen by no more than 1 percent for the southern-most regions following trade reforms.

In India, Ural Marchand (2012) finds significant regional variation in the pass-through elasticities across rural and urban localities. In rural India, the most conservative effects of tariff pass-through on domestic prices range from 33 to 49 percent versus a more elastic range of between 64 and 68 percent in urban areas. Not coincidentally then, welfare gains in urban areas are much higher than those in rural areas.

Market power of intermediaries. Traders who possess market power may not allow tariff reductions to be fully reflected in prices because they find it optimal to absorb a portion of the price effect. This in turn has important implications for the magnitude of intranational barriers to trade and the incidence of trade. In Sub-Saharan Africa, Atkin and Donaldson (2015) find that intermediaries capture much of the surplus from trade liberalization and that their share is even higher in distant locations, suggesting that remote consumers see only a small part of the gains from falling international trade barriers.

Domestic market structure. The role of market structure—the size of the private or public sector in the domestic economy—also determines the tariff pass-through and ultimately the incidence of changes in tariffs on household welfare. A heavily regulated domestic industry could distort pass-through to consumers, whereas a more competitive private sector could accelerate this. Han et al. (2016) analyze how the structure of markets can determine the tariff pass-through in China. They find that a higher share of private sector enterprises in Chinese cities is associated with higher levels of tariff pass-through rates. In a city where all enterprises are state-owned, the average pass-through rate is 22 percent, whereas a city with an average-sized private sector has a tariff pass-through rate of about 31 percent.

Conclusion

Overall, substantial methodological advances in the literature have strengthened our ability to understand the complex relationship between trade, labor income, and consumption at the subnational level within countries. Trade clearly has brought overall gains to households and is critical to the reduction of poverty, but labor market and consumption gains have been concentrated in some regions and groups.

In addition, the evidence base is limited to a few countries, and several knowledge gaps remain despite significant advances in the understanding of the ex post and ex ante impacts of trade shocks. The disproportionate emphasis on examining the distributional impacts of trade on labor markets (wages and employment) is clearly evident, while impacts on consumer prices remain relatively less understood because of data limitations. Key gaps remain in our understanding of how trade shocks affect consumption and local labor markets (especially in low-income countries) and of short-term and long-term transitional dynamics following a trade shock. Also understudied, despite the expanding evidence base in recent decades, is the local impact of higher exports as opposed to the impact of import competition and lower tariffs. Some other areas for which evidence needs to be expanded include (a) the role of informal employment as a key adjustment mechanism, (b) gendered labor market outcomes, and (c) distributional impacts propagated through global value chains.

As chapter 3 shows, World Bank teams have contributed to filling some of these gaps by advancing backward- and forward-looking methodological approaches. These approaches are complementary and can be grouped into three broad categories: (a) backward-looking reduced-form analysis using and structural analysis detailed micro data to study local labor market impacts, (b) forward-looking partial equilibrium analysis using the HIT database, and (c) forward-looking general equilibrium analysis using the Computable General Equilibrium–Global Income Distribution Dynamics (CGE-GIDD) tool.

- To start with, backward-looking analysis assesses the impact of changes in trade on outcomes such as employment, wages, informality across time, regions, and demographic characteristics such as age and skill level. More complex analysis can account for mobility costs and adjustment mechanisms.

- The HIT approach captures the ex ante short-term impacts of tariff liberalization and allows for granularity of outcomes across households given changes in tariffs at the product level. It incorporates detailed consumption patterns at the household level and is best equipped to estimate short-term impacts on consumption.

- The CGE-GIDD approach allows for the ex ante medium- and long-term assessment of the impacts of trade policy reforms, because the model includes input-output relationships across sectors, differences across countries in the sectoral compositions of their economies, and bilateral trade relationships. It also imposes economic consistency, because changes across all variables add up to the total productive capacity within the economy consistent with factors of production and sectoral productivity. The impacts on households and regions are generated in microsimulations consistent with the aggregate shocks.

In the next chapter, we delve deeper into some of the empirical gaps identified in this chapter and then use backward- and forward-looking approaches described in this chapter to analyze the within-country impacts of trade on labor income and consumption for five countries through the lens of specific policy questions, data availability, and time frame. Through these case studies, we also build on the evidence by filling in knowledge gaps and testing some of our key findings in new country contexts.

Notes

1. Early theoretical foundations for understanding distributional implications of trade lie in the widely discussed Heckscher-Ohlin (H-O) model with its companion Stolper-Samuelson (S-S) theorem (Stolper and Samuelson 1941), which predicts that with perfect factor mobility greater integration raises the real returns to the relatively common factor such as unskilled labor in developing countries. Many empirical studies assessing the validity of the S-S theorem, however, find mixed results. Some studies in Latin America show that, contrary to the prediction of the S-S theorem, wage inequality rose (Hanson 2003; López-Calva and Lustig 2010). Some other studies provide support to the S-S theorem (Robertson 2004). In summary, the earlier literature has provided inconsistent and mixed results, whereas new data and tools allow exploring the mechanisms and channels through which trade impacts distribution.

2. In the case of Mexico, Robertson (2004) shows that, following substantial tariff reductions as part of the General Agreement on Tariffs and Trade reforms in 1986, the unskilled sector took the hardest hit in terms of wages and employment in the short run, contrary to the predictions of the S-S theorem (Stolper and Samuelson 1941). This trending increase in wage inequality that occurred in the short term, however, reversed itself after deeper integration reforms in the 1990s driven by a decline in relative wages of skilled workers.

3. It is important to differentiate between ex post general equilibrium studies and ex ante computable general equilibrium (CGE) simulation studies projecting future outcomes. A review of these can be found in Cirera, Willenbockel, and Lakshman (2014), who compare the findings of ex post econometric studies with ex ante CGE simulation studies. In the case of the latter, a reallocation of factors is assumed to happen, resulting in generally positive impacts from trade liberalization on employment.

4. As discussed in detail by Artuç and McLaren (2015), most studies in the 1990s and early 2000s analyze the effect of trade changes on labor based on the physical or human capital of workers in line with the S-S theorem. As the understanding of the distributional impacts of trade became more dynamic, other factors like industry affiliation and the age of workers became more important. Thus, several studies in the mid 2000s take approaches that analyze impact on workers based on industry of employment (such as Artuç, Chaudhuri, and McLaren 2010; Pavcnik et al. 2004) and age (such as Artuç 2012). Others focus on occupations (such as Autor, Levy, and Murnane 2003; Ebenstein et al. 2014).

5. Hoekman and Porto (2010) provide an overview of adjustment costs to trade in low-income countries with large informal and agricultural that go beyond labor costs.

6. Atkin and Khandelwal (2020) provide a detailed review of literature that assesses how distortions such as the presence of weak institutions and market failures alter the impacts of trade reforms in developed and developing countries.

References

Acemoglu, Daron, David Autor, David Dorn, Gordon Hanson, and Brendan Price. 2016. "Import Competition and the Great US Employment Sag of the 2000s." *Journal of Labor Economics* 34 (S1): S141–98.

Adão, Rodrigo. 2016, "Worker Heterogeneity, Wage Inequality, and International Trade: Theory and Evidence from Brazil." Working paper, Massachusetts Institute of Technology, Cambridge, MA.

Adão, Rodrigo, Costas Arkolakis, and Federico Esposito. 2019. "Spatial Linkages, Global Shocks, and Local Labor Markets: Theory and Evidence." Discussion Paper 2163, Cowles Foundation for Research in Economics, Yale University, New Haven, CT.

Agustina, Fina. 2018. "Import Competition and Local Labor Markets: the Case of Indonesia." *Economic Journal of Emerging Markets* 10 (2): 177–86.

Arias, Javier, Erhan Artuç, Daniel Lederman, and Diego Rojas. 2018. "Trade, Informal Employment, and Labor Adjustment Costs." *Journal of Development Economics.* 133 (C): 396–414.

Artuç, Erhan, 2012. "Workers' Age and the Impact of Trade Shocks." Policy Research Working Paper 6035, World Bank, Washington, DC.

Artuç, Erhan, Shubham Chaudhuri, and John McLaren. 2010. "Trade Shocks and Labor Adjustment: A Structural Empirical Approach." *American Economic Review,* 100 (3): 1008–45.

Artuç, Erhan, Gladys Lopez-Acevedo, Raymond Robertson, and Daniel Samaan. 2019. *Exports to Jobs: Boosting the Gains from Trade in South Asia.* Washington, DC: World Bank.

Artuç, Erhan, and John McLaren. 2010. "A Structural Empirical Approach to Trade Shocks and Labor Adjustment: An Application to Turkey." In *Trade Adjustment Costs in Developing Countries and*

Adjustment Impacts of Trade Policy: Impacts, Determinants, and Policy Responses, edited by Bernard Hoekman and Guido Porto. Washington, DC: World Bank.

Artuç, Erhan, and John McLaren. 2015. "Trade Policy and Wage Inequality: A Structural Analysis with Occupational and Sectoral Mobility." *Journal of International Economics* 97 (2) 278–94.

Artuç, Erhan, Guido Porto, and Bob Rijkers. 2019. "Household Impacts of Tariffs: Data and Results from Agricultural Trade Protection." Policy Research Working Paper 9045, World Bank, Washington, DC.

Asquith, Brian, Sanjana Goswami, David Neumark, and Antonio Rodriguez-Lopez. 2017. "US Job Flows and the China Shock." Working Paper 24080, National Bureau of Economic Research, Cambridge, MA.

Atkin, Dave, and Dave Donaldson. 2015. "Who's Getting Globalized? The Size and Implications of Intranational Trade Costs." Working Paper 21439, National Bureau of Economic Research, Cambridge, MA.

Atkin, David, Benjamin Faber, and Marco Gonzalez-Navarro. 2018. "Retail Globalization and Household Welfare: Evidence from Mexico." *Journal of Political Economy* 126 (1): 1–73.

Atkin, David, and Amit K. Khandelwal. 2020. "How Distortions Alter the Impacts of International Trade in Developing Countries." *Annual Review of Economics* 12 (1): 213–38.

Autor, David, David Dorn, and Gordon H. Hanson. 2013. "The China Syndrome: Local Labor Market Effects of Import Competition in the United States." *American Economic Review* 103 (6): 2121–68.

Autor, David H., David Dorn, and Gordon H. Hanson. 2016. "The China Shock: Learning from Labor-Market Adjustment to Large Changes in Trade." *Annual Review of Economics* 8: 205–40.

Autor, David, David Dorn, Gordon H. Hanson, and Jae Song. 2014. "Trade Adjustment: Worker-Level Evidence." *Quarterly Journal of* Economics 129 (4): 1799–860.

Autor, David, Frank Levy, and Richard J. Murnane. 2003. "The Skill Content of Recent Technological Change: An Empirical Exploration." *Quarterly Journal of Economics* 118 (4): 1279–333.

Banerjee, Abhijit, and Andrew Newman. 2004. "Inequality, Growth and Trade Policy." Massachusetts Institute of Technology, Department of Economics and University College London, Department of Economics.

Bernard, Andrew, Teresa Fort, Valerie Smeets, and Frederic Warzynski. 2020. "Heterogeneous Globalization: Offshoring and Reorganization." Working Paper 26854, National Bureau of Economic Research, Cambridge, MA.

Beyer, Harald, Patricio Rojas, and Rodrigo Vergara. 1999. "Trade Liberalization and Wage Inequality." *Journal of Development Economics* 59 (1):103–23.

Bloom, Nicholas, Andre Kurmann, Kyle Handley, Philip Luck. 2019. "The Impact of Chinese Trade on US Employment: The Good, the Bad, and the Apocryphal." Meeting Paper 1433, Society for Economic Dynamics, St. Louis, MO.

Borusyak, Kirill, and Xavier Jaravel. 2018. "The Distributional Effects of Trade: Theory and Evidence from the United States." Meeting Paper 284, Society for Economic Dynamics, St. Louis, MO.

Bosch, Mariano, Edwin Goni, and William Maloney. 2012. "Trade Liberalization, Labor Reforms and Formal-Informal Employment Dynamics." *Labor Economics* 19 (5): 653–67.

Brummund, Peter, and Laura Connolly. 2019. "Labor Market Adjustments to Trade with China: The Case of Brazil." University of Alabama, Tuscaloosa.

Cali, Massimiliano, Taufik Hidayat, and Claire Hollweg. 2019. "What Is Behind Labor Mobility Costs? Evidence from Indonesia." Background paper for *Time to ACT*, World Bank, Washington, DC.

Caliendo, Lorenzo, Maximiliano Dvorkin, and Fernando Parro. 2019. "Trade and Labor Market Dynamics: General Equilibrium Analysis of the China Trade Shock." *Econometrica* 87 (3): 741–835.

Caliendo, Lorenzo, and Fernando Parro. 2015. "Estimates of the Trade and Welfare Effects of NAFTA." *Review of Economic Studies* 82 (1): 1–44.

Cirera, Xavier, Dirk Willenbockel, and Rajith W. D. Lakshman. 2014. "Evidence on the Impact of Tariff Reductions on Employment in Developing Countries: A Systematic Review." *Journal of Economic Surveys* 28 (3): 449–71.

Cosar, A. Kerem. 2013. "Adjusting to Trade Liberalization: Reallocation and Labor Market Policies." Booth School of Business, University of Chicago. http://economics.yale.edu/sites /default/files /files/Workshops-Seminars/International-Trade/cosar-101103.pdf.

Currie, Janet, and Ann Harrison. 1997. "Sharing the Costs: The Impact of Trade Reform on Capital and Labor in Morocco." *Journal of Labor Economics* 15 (3): S44–71.

Davidson, Carl, and Steven J. Matusz. 2004. *International Trade and Labor Markets: Theory, Evidence, and Policy Implication.* Kalamazoo MI: W. E. Upjohn Institute for Employment Research.

Deaton, Angus. 1989. "Rice Prices and Income Distribution in Thailand: A Nonparametric Analysis." *Economic Journal* 99 (395): 1–37.

Dix-Carneiro, Rafael. 2014. "Trade Liberalization and Labor Market Dynamics." *Econometrica* 82 (3): 825–85.

Dix-Carneiro, Rafael, Pinelopi Goldberg, Costas Meghir, and Gabriel Ulyssea. 2021. "Trade and Informality in the Presence of Labor Market Frictions and Regulations." Working Paper 28391, National Bureau of Economic Research, Cambridge, MA.

Dix-Carneiro, Rafael, and Brian K. Kovak. 2015. "Trade Liberalization and the Skill Premium: A Local Labor Markets Approach." *American Economic Review* 105 (5):551–57.

Dix-Carneiro, Rafael, and Brian K. Kovak. 2017. "Trade Liberalization and Regional Dynamics." *American Economic Review* 107 (10): 2908–46.

Dix-Carneiro, Rafael, and Brian K. Kovak. 2019. "Margins of Labor Market Adjustment to Trade." *Journal of International Economics* 117 (C): 125–42.

Ebenstein, Avraham, Ann. E. Harrison, Margaret S. McMillan, and Shannon Phillips. 2014. "Estimating the Impact of Trade and Offshoring on American Workers Using the Current Population Surveys." *Review of Economics and Statistics* 96 (4): 581–95.

Edmonds, Eric, Nina Pavcnik, and Petia Topalova. 2007. "Trade Adjustment and Human Capital Investment: Evidence from Indian Tariff Reform." Working Paper 07/94, International Monetary Fund, Washington, DC. https://papers.ssrn.com/sol3/papers.cfm?abstract_id=986822.

Erten, Bilge, and Jessica Leight. 2019. "Exporting out of Agriculture: The Impact of WTO Accession on Structural Transformation in China." *Review of Economics and Statistics* 103 (2): 1–46.

Erten, Bilge, Jessica Leight, and Fiona Tregenna. 2019. "Trade Liberalization and Local Labor Market Adjustment in South Africa." *Journal of International Economics* 118 (C): 448–67.

Faber, Benjamin. 2014. "Trade Liberalization, the Price of Quality, and Inequality: Evidence from Mexican Store Prices." Working paper, University of California at Berkeley. https://eml.berkeley .edu/~faberb/Mexico.pdf.

Fajgelbaum, Pablo D., and Amit K. Khandelwal. 2016. "Measuring the Unequal Gains from Trade." *Quarterly Journal of Economics* 131 (3): 1113–80.

Fan, Jingting. 2019. "Internal Geography, Labor Mobility, and the Distributional Impacts of Trade." *American Economic Journal: Macroeconomics* 11 (3): 252–88.

Feenstra, Robert, and Gordon Hanson. 2001. "Global Production Sharing and Rising Inequality: A Survey of Trade and Wages." Working Paper 8372, National Bureau of Economic Research, Cambridge, MA.

Feenstra, Robert, Hong Ma, and Yuan Xu. 2017a. "US Exports and Employment." Working Paper 24056, National Bureau of Economic Research, Cambridge, MA.

Feenstra, Robert, and Akira Sasahara. 2017. "The 'China Shock,' Exports and US Employment: A Global Input-Output Analysis." Working Paper 24022, National Bureau of Economic Research, Cambridge, MA.

Galle, Simon, Andrés Rodríguez-Clare, and Moises Yi. 2017. "Slicing the Pie: Quantifying the Aggregate and Distributional Effects of Trade." Working Paper 23737, National Bureau of Economic Research, Cambridge, MA.

Góes, Carlos, Alexandre Messa, Carlos Pio, Leoni, Eduardo, and Luis Gustavo. 2019. "Trade Liberalization and Active Labor Market Policies." In *Brazil: Boom, Bust and the Road to Recovery*, edited by Antonio Spilimbergo and Krishna Srinivasan, Washington, DC: International Monetary Fund.

Goldberg, Pinelopi, and Nina Pavcnik. 2007a. "Distributional Effects of Globalization in Developing Countries." *Journal of Economic Literature* 45 (1): 39–82.

Goldberg, Pinelopi, and Nina Pavcnik. 2007b. "The Effects of the Colombian Trade Liberalization on Urban Poverty." *Globalization and Poverty* 3: 241–90.

Gonzaga, Gustavo, Naércio Menezes Filho, and Cristina Terra. 2006. "Trade Liberalization and the Evolution of Skill Earnings Differentials in Brazil." *Journal of International Economics.* 68 (2): 345–67.

Goutam, Prodyumna, Italo A. Gutierrez, Krishna B. Kumar, and Shanthi Nataraj. 2017. "Does Informal Employment Respond to Growth Opportunities? Trade-Based Evidence from Bangladesh." Working Paper WR-1198, RAND Corporation, Washington, DC.

Han, Jun, Runjuan Liu, Beyza Ural, and Junsen Zhang. 2016. "Market Structure, Imperfect Tariff Pass-Through, and Household Welfare in Urban China." *Journal of International Economics* 100 (C): 220–32.

Hanson, Gordon. 2003 "What Has Happened to Wages in Mexico Since NAFTA?" Working Paper 9563, National Bureau of Economic Research, Cambridge, MA.

Harrison, Ann E., John McLaren, and Margaret McMillan. 2011. "Recent Perspectives on Trade and Inequality." Policy Research Working Paper 5754, World Bank, Washington, DC.

Hasan, Rana, Devashish Mitra, Priya Ranjan, and Reshad N. Ahsan. 2012. "Trade Liberalization and Unemployment: Theory and Evidence from India." *Journal of Development Economics* 97 (2): 269–80.

Hasan, Rana, Devashish Mitra, and Beyza P. Ural. 2007. "Trade Liberalization, Labor-Market Institutions, and Poverty Reduction: Evidence from Indian States." *India Policy Forum* 3 (1): 71–122.

Hoekman, Bernard, and Guido Porto, eds. 2010. *Trade Adjustment Costs in Developing Countries: Impacts, Determinants and Policy Responses*. Washington, DC: World Bank.

Kambourov, Gueorgui. 2009. "Labor Market Regulations and the Sectoral Reallocation of Workers: The Case of Trade Reforms." *Review of Economic Studies* 76 (4): 1321–58.

Kis-Katos, Krisztina, Janneke Pieters, and Robert Sparrow. 2018. "Globalization and Social Change: Gender-Specific Effects of Trade Liberalization in Indonesia." *IMF Economic Review* 66 (4): 763–93.

Kis-Katos, Krisztina, and Robert Sparrow. 2015. "Poverty, Labor Markets, and Trade Liberalization in Indonesia." *Journal of Development Economics* 117 (C): 94–106.

Kokas, D. and J. Engle. Forthcoming. "Distributional Impact of Trade Reforms: A Survey of Theory, Evidence and Policy."

Kovak, Brian K. 2010. "Regional Labor Market Effects of Trade Policy: Evidence from Brazilian Liberalization." Working Paper 605, Research Seminar in International Economics, University of Michigan, Ann Arbor.

Kovak, Brian K. 2013. "Regional Effects of Trade Reform: What Is the Correct Measure of Liberalization?" *American Economic Review* 103 (5): 1960–76.

López-Calva, Luis, and Nora Lustig, eds. 2010. *Declining Inequality in Latin America a Decade of Progress*. Washington, DC: Brookings Institution Press.

Matusz, Steven J., and David G. Tarr. 1999. "Adjusting to Trade Policy Reform." Michigan State University, East Lansing. https://ssrn.com/abstract=597268.

Matusz, Steven J., and David Tarr. 2000. "Adjusting to Trade Liberalization." In *Economic Policy Reform: The Second Stage*, edited by Anne O. Krueger. Chicago: University of Chicago Press.

McCaig, Brian, and Nina Pavcnik. 2018. "Export Markets and Labor Allocation in a Low-Income Country." *American Economic Review* 108 (7): 1899–941.

McCulloch, Neil, L. Alan Winters, and Xavier Cirera. 2001. *Trade Liberalization and Poverty: A Handbook*. London: Center for Economic Policy Research.

McLaren, John. 2017. "Globalization and Labor Market Dynamics." *Annual Review of Economics* 9: 177–200.

Menezes-Filho, Naercio, and Marc-Andreas Muendler. 2011. "Labor Reallocation in Response to Trade Reform." Working Paper 17372, National Bureau of Economic Research, Cambridge, MA.

Milanovic, Branko, and Lyn Squire. 2007. "Does Tariff Liberalization Increase Wage Inequality? Some Empirical Evidence." *Globalization and Poverty* 3: 143–82.

Monte, Ferdinando. 2015. "The Local Incidence of Trade Shocks." Working Paper, Georgetown University, Washington, DC. https://ssrn.com/abstract=2337270 or http://dx.doi.org/10.2139/ssrn.2337270.

Morten, Melanie, and Jacqueline Oliveira. 2016. "Paving the Way to Development: Costly Migration and Labor Market Integration." Working Paper 22158, National Bureau of Economic Research, Cambridge, MA.

Nicita, Alessandro. 2009. "The Price Effect of Tariff Liberalization: Measuring the Impact on Household Welfare." *Journal of Development Economics* 89 (1): 19–27.

Nicita, Alessandro, Marcelo Olarreaga, and Guido Porto. 2014. "Pro-Poor Trade Policy in Sub-Saharan Africa." *Journal of International Economics* 92 (2): 252–65.

Ortiz-Ospina E., and D. Beltekian. 2018. Trade and Globalization, Our World in Data.https://www.ourworldindata.org/trade-and-globalization.

Papageorgiou, Demetris, Armeane M. Choksi, and Michael Michaely, eds. 1990. *Liberalizing Foreign Trade: Lessons of Experience in the Developing World*. Oxford, UK: Blackwell Publishing.

Pavcnik, Nina. 2017. "The Impact of Trade on Inequality in Developing Countries." CEPR Discussion Papers 12331.

Pavcnik, Nina, Andreas Blom, Pinelopi Goldberg, and Norbert Schady. 2004. "Trade Liberalization and Industry Wage Structure: Evidence from Brazil." *World Bank Economic Review* 18 (3): 319–44.

Pierce, Justin R., and Peter K. Schott. 2016. "The Surprisingly Swift Decline of US Manufacturing Employment." *American Economic Review* 106 (7): 1632–62.

Ponczek, Vladimir, and Gabriel Ulyssea. 2018. "Is Informality an Employment Buffer? Evidence from the Trade Liberalization in Brazil." Working paper, Brazilian School of Public and Business Administration, Fundação Getulio Vargas, Rio de Janeiro, Brazil.

Porto, Guido. 2006. "Using Survey Data to Assess the Distributional Effects of Trade Policy." *Journal of International Economics* 70 (1): 140–60.

Revenga, Ana L. 1992. "Exporting Jobs? The Impact of Import Competition on Employment and Wages in U.S. Manufacturing." *Quarterly Journal of Economics* 107 (1): 255–84.

Revenga, Ana, 1997. "Employment and Wage Effects of Trade Liberalization: The Case of Mexican Manufacturing." *Journal of Labor Economics* 15 (3): 20–43.

Ritter, Moritz. 2012. "Offshoring and Occupational Specificity of Human Capital." DETU Working Paper 1207, Department of Economics, Temple University, Philadelphia.

Robertson, Raymond. 2004. "Relative Prices and Wage Inequality: Evidence from Mexico." *Journal of International Economics* 64 (2): 387–409.

Robertson, Raymond. 2018. "Effects of Regulating International Trade on Firms and Workers." Institute of Labor Economics (IZA), Bonn, Germany. https://wol.iza.org/uploads/articles/439/pdfs/effects-of-regulating-international-trade-on-firms-and-workers.pdf.

Rojas-Vallejos, Jorge, and Stephen J. Turnovsky. 2017. "Tariff Reduction and Income Inequality: Some Empirical Evidence." *Open Economies Review* 28 (4): 603–31.

Sarra, Ben Yahmed, and Pamela Bombarda. 2018. "Gender, Informal Employment and Trade Liberalization in Mexico." Discussion Paper 18-028, Center for European Economic Research (ZEW).

Stolper, Wolfgang F., and Paul A. Samuelson. 1941. "Protection and Real Wages." *Review of Economic Studies* 9 (1): 58–73.

Topalova, Petia. 2007. "Trade Liberalization, Poverty and Inequality: Evidence from Indian Districts." *Globalization and Poverty* 3: 291–336.

Topalova, Petia. 2010. "Factor Immobility and Regional Impacts of Trade Liberalization: Evidence on Poverty from India." *American Economic Journal: Applied Economics* 2 (4): 1–41.

Ural Marchand, Beyza. 2012. "Tariff Pass-Through and the Distributional Effects of Trade Liberalization." *Journal of Development Economics* 99 (2): 265–81.

Ural Marchand, Beyza. 2017. "How does international trade affect household welfare?" IZA World of Labor 2017: 378 doi: 10.15185/izawol.378.

Wang, Zhi, Shang-Jin Wei, Xinding Yu, and Kunfu Zhu. 2018. "Reexamining the Effects of Trading with China on Local Labor Markets: A Supply Chain Perspective." Working Paper 24886, National Bureau of Economic Research, Cambridge, MA.

Wood, Adrian. 1997. "Openness and Wage Inequality in Developing Countries: The Latin American Challenge to East Asian Conventional Wisdom." *World Bank Economic Review* 11 (1): 33–57.

World Bank. 2020. *World Development Report 2020: Trading for Development in the Age of Global Value Chains.* Washington, DC: World Bank.

Xu, Yuan, Hong Ma, and Robert C. Feenstra. 2019. "Magnification of the 'China Shock' through the U.S. Housing Market." Working Paper 26432, National Bureau of Economic Research, Cambridge, MA.

Zi, Yuan. 2018. *Trade Liberalization and the Hukou System of the People's Republic of China: How Migration Frictions Can Amplify the Unequal Gains from Trade.* Working Paper 887, Asian Development Bank Institute, Tokyo.

3. Lessons from Recent Cases of Trade Reforms in Developing Countries

Key Messages

- This report synthesizes five case studies of low- and middle-income countries—Mexico, Bangladesh, South Africa, Brazil, and Sri Lanka—to fill in empirical gaps relating to trade reforms and their impact on local labor markets, consumption, and distributional outcomes.

- How would subnational effects of trade reforms play out over time? In South Africa, long-term adverse effects are strongest in municipalities that include former homelands and a higher share of the black population, which reflects historically low labor mobility across regions, sectors, and occupations. In Bangladesh, though, trade-related regional differences in wages and informality are more temporary because of relatively low migration barriers and the apparel-specific nature of the export shock.

- How would higher exports affect incomes and jobs at the subnational level? In Mexico, higher exports since the North American Free Trade Agreement (NAFTA) have had a large and positive impact on total labor incomes, but their impacts on poverty reduction and household incomes per capita have been negligible because of higher return migration rates and weak linkages between tradable and nontradable sectors. In Brazil, the manufacturing sector, which like other sectors benefits from lower export costs, attracts workers from other industries within the same microregion because of the prohibitively large interregional moving costs.

- How would policy reforms affect jobs at the subnational level? In Sri Lanka, for example, lower trade barriers would lead to lower poverty and a faster expansion of gross domestic product and international trade but greater wage inequality and a concentration of economic activity in urban areas.

- Overall, these country cases highlight different political and economic dynamics that drive the differences in how trade reforms affect each country's welfare outcomes. They offer insights that could inform policies to help avoid or mitigate some of the negative impacts from trade reforms ex ante and distribute the benefits of trade more broadly.

Introduction

In recent decades, there have been substantial advances in our understanding of the theoretical and empirical relationship between aggregate and distributional impacts of trade reforms on welfare (see chapter 2). These advances have shown how impacts can vary spatially (at the local or national level) and temporally (in .the short and long term). Although the empirical literature analyzing the distributional impacts of trade has expanded, evidence of subnational variations in impacts remains concentrated in a few countries. Even so, these studies offer some key empirical lessons.

The subnational effects of trade shocks can be large, can disproportionately affect some localities more than others depending on their exposure to such shocks, and may be negative or positive depending on the type of shock. In Brazil and India, import competition has triggered a large decline in wages and employment, and an increase in informality in import-competing regions relative to others. In China, India, and Vietnam, higher exports have reduced poverty, improved wages, and spurred a reallocation of labor from informal to formal jobs in localities more exposed to higher exports.

Negative or positive subnational impacts on employment and wages persist over time in localities with greater exposure. Recent work finds wage and employment declines in regions more exposed to import competition to be more pronounced 20 years after the trade reforms in Brazil than they had been after 10 years (Dix-Carneiro and Kovak 2017). Similarly, districts in India that experienced greater exposure to a rise in exports tended to experience sustained increases in wages and reductions in informality.

Not surprisingly, researchers find that these costs are in part driven by multiple barriers to mobility. Dix-Carneiro (2014) shows that, in Brazil, a large part of the switching cost is caused by the low transferability of human capital, a finding that others have substantiated. In some other countries, adjustment costs are driven by actual moving costs needed to find or start a new job. In Chile, China, and Mexico, labor market regulations and policies related to housing drive these costs higher and depress gains from trade.

Informal employment can be an important channel of adjustment for workers in emerging economies, regardless of the type of trade shock they are exposed to. In Brazil, there has been a rise in informality in areas more exposed to tariff reductions in the medium term. In contrast, research on India and Vietnam highlights a pattern of workers shifting from informal to formal employment in areas more exposed to greater export orientation.

Trade liberalization can typically favor the poor through lower prices, unlike income losses, which are more concentrated. While understudied, existing evidence consistently suggests pro-poor consumption gains from trade reforms across countries. This is not surprising because traded goods form a significant share of a low-income household budget compared to that of nontraded goods or services, especially in emerging economies (Artuç et al. 2020).

Benefits from lower prices may not fully pass through to consumers depending on factors like geographic characteristics of localities, efficiency of product markets, and markups (Ural Marchand 2012). Evidence from Ethiopia and Nigeria shows that intermediaries capture the majority of the surplus (Atkin and Donaldson 2015).

If we are to ensure that gains from trade are more broadly distributed going forward, however, we need to better understand the connections between changes in trade and (a) local labor market impacts, (b) consumption channel impacts, and (c) ultimate distributional impacts. Specifically, many important questions are still left unanswered.

- To what extent do the long-lasting income impacts of trade reforms that are observed in Brazil also apply to other emerging economies and institutional settings, and are there specific components of adjustment costs that could lead to persistent income impacts?

- Beyond wages and employment, are there any other important channels of adjustment in labor markets? Is informal employment a key adjustment mechanism in emerging economies?

- What are the local labor market effects of expanding exports to rich countries on workers from emerging economies? Which groups gain or lose more?

- What are the consumption and income impacts in low-income countries of higher exports to rich countries? And how do these effects vary across the income distribution?

To shed more light on these questions, this report synthesizes five case studies of low- and middle-income countries—Mexico, Bangladesh, South Africa, Brazil, and Sri Lanka—to test emerging empirical lessons and fill in empirical gaps. These studies include countries that have (a) undergone significant trade reforms in the past two decades, (b) evidence of geographical concentration of production and sluggish mobility across regions, (c) broad country coverage in terms of both regions and level of development, and (d) available data for an econometric analysis of local labor market impacts.

The studies on Bangladesh and South Africa test whether the subnational effects of trade reforms persist over time (as has been found for Brazil) and whether some communities are more affected than others. The study on Bangladesh also examines whether the informal economy acted an a vital adjustment channel for workers in response to trade shocks. The studies on Bangladesh, Brazil, and Mexico expand the underdeveloped evidence base documenting the local distributional impacts of exports. And the study on Sri Lanka aims to unpack the potential impacts of broad trade policy reforms on employment at the subnational level. A variety of data and models have been applied to answer these questions (appendix A).

Overall, we find that there are very different political and economic dynamics in the five countries, including sector-specific export shocks in Bangladesh, low mobility by historically disadvantaged groups in South Africa, high mobility costs in Brazil, and greater return migration and weak economic linkages in Mexico. All these insights can help policy makers craft policies to help avoid or mitigate some of the negative impacts from trade reforms ex ante and distribute gains from trade more broadly.

Mexico: How Rising Exports Affect Local Poverty and Inequality

Mexico joined the General Agreement on Tariffs and Trade (GATT) in 1986 and NAFTA in 1994, which led to substantial tariff reductions both globally and regionally, greater export orientation, and the country's diversification away from oil. Exports of goods and services shot up from US$96.7 million in 1990 to US$480 billion in 2018, from 18.7 percent of gross domestic product (GDP) to 39.2 percent. Moreover, since 2004, most of its exports (70 to 80 percent) have gone to the United States. Mexico has nonetheless underperformed in terms of growth, inclusion, and poverty reduction compared to its peers (World Bank 2019).

Between 2004 and 2014 (the period covered by this study), poverty in Mexico declined by 4 percentage points, (from 37.6 to 33.6 percent), while it declined by nearly 17 percentage points, from 41.3 to 24.4 percent (US$5.50 per day per capita poverty line, 2011 purchasing power parity) in Latin America and the Caribbean. Almost half of the decline in poverty in Mexico is explained by redistribution (partially due to the shift from general subsidies to targeted and conditional transfers) rather than by economic growth, despite the expansion in trade over the period. In Latin America, by contrast, redistribution explains only about 20 percent of the decline, whereas economic growth accounted for nearly 80 percent of the reduction in poverty, driven in part by the commodity boom that started in 2003 and lasted until 2014.

These poverty declines were relatively small compared to those of other countries typically mentioned as examples of successful export-led growth. Vietnam, whose export-to-GDP ratio increased from 54.7 to 70.3 percent between 2002 and 2008, experienced a substantial reduction in poverty: the share of people living on less than US$3.20 a day declined from about 70.8 to 46.8 percent.

Why did increasing exports not translate into lower poverty and higher income growth in Mexico? "Tracing the Local Impacts of Exports on Poverty and Inequality in Mexico" by Rodríguez-Castelán, Vazquez, and Winkler (2020) offers insight on this question by exploiting variations in export growth across Mexican municipalities between 2004 and 2014 to identify the impacts on poverty and inequality at the municipal level. Understanding the impacts of trade at the local level is crucial in a context such as Mexico because, as shown in this study, about 75 percent of total inequality is explained by inequality within the municipality, rather than between municipalities.

Identifying the impacts of exports on poverty and inequality is challenging because there are a variety of factors (several of which are unobservable to researchers) that affect international trade and the income distribution and can thus generate spurious correlations between both sets of outcomes. Even though municipalities with higher levels of exports are richer and more unequal, for example (see figure 3.1), this does not necessarily imply that the former explains the latter. To overcome this challenge, this case study pursues an empirical strategy that isolates changes in exports at the local level from other changes that may introduce a bias in the estimates.

The results show that Mexico's increase in exports to richer countries did not necessarily lead to better welfare indicators at the local level. Although exports, as expected, have a large and positive impact on total labor incomes, their impacts on poverty reduction and household incomes per capita are negligible. Several factors mitigate their potential effect on poverty rates and average incomes.

FIGURE 3.1 **Municipalities with Higher Exports Have Less Poverty, Have Higher Incomes, and Are More Unequal**

Poverty, per capita incomes, and inequality in municipalities with relatively high and low levels of exports, 2015

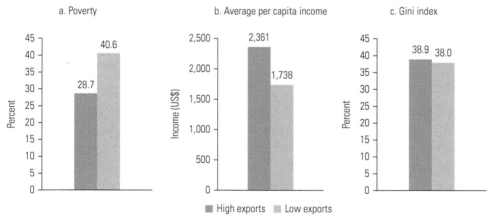

Source: Original calculations for this publication are based on household surveys (poverty, average per capita income, and Gini), population census (workers), and customs data (exports).

Note: The sample is restricted to the urban and semiurban municipalities with complete data. A municipality has relatively high (low) exports if its exports-to-workers ratio for 2000 is above (below) the median at the municipality level. Poverty is measured as the Foster-Greer-Thorbecke (0) index with the official food poverty line. Monetary values are in real terms at 2014 prices and were deflated using the average National Consumer Price Index (base December 2010). Poverty, average per capita income, and the Gini index are computed as simple averages across municipalities.

- Exports led to both a positive labor demand and a labor supply shock. In particular, although exports increased the total labor income at the local level, they also increased labor force participation and the size of the working-age population, resulting in no significant changes in labor income per worker.
- Higher exports led to lower out-migration and higher inflows of return migrants from both the United States and other Mexican municipalities, which led to an increase in the size of the working-age population, as well as a change in its composition. Exports increase the number of unskilled workers at the municipal level disproportionately, which tends to raise poverty and inequality.
- An increase in exports led to a decline in nonlabor income by reducing the volume of remittances. These results are consistent with the hypothesis put forward by Robertson (2007), who argues that the lack of positive labor market impacts from trade integration could partly be explained by migration.

It should be mentioned, however, that, even though the expected impacts of exports on welfare at the local level were negligible, this does not imply that the average individual in Mexico did not see any gains. Take, for example, a case in which a municipality's exports did not affect the incomes of current residents but attracted migrants who would have been worse off otherwise at their previous location. The fact that labor mobility was very responsive to exports means that this mechanism cannot be discarded.

The study also finds that, although exports did not have a significant effect on the level of household incomes per capita, they do affect relative incomes in a progressive way. A 10 percent increase in the export-to-worker ratio reduces income inequality as measured by the Gini coefficient by 0.17 points (using a 0 to 100 scale). The fact that exports have a progressive impact on incomes at the local level contrasts with findings of plant-level studies that exports increase wage inequality within plants and industries.

On the policy front, these findings suggest that, if developing countries want to fully reap the benefits of greater integration with rich economies, it is essential to foster stronger links between the tradᵒable and nontradable sectors so that the positive effects of exports spread beyond the former. Specifically, critical bottlenecks contribute to weak linkages between NAFTA export-oriented firms in Mexico's northern and central states and a large share of low-productivity, often informal firms not linked to those global value chains (World Bank 2019). These bottlenecks included the following:

- *Significant obstacles to competition.* As of 2013, product market regulations were relatively restrictive compared with other Organisation for Economic Co-operation and Development countries. Coupled with other distortions,

The Distributional Impacts of Trade

such barriers protect incumbent firms and prevent the entry of newcomers. Regulatory barriers to competition at the local level, often linked to powerful vested interests, tend to be dispersed across sectors and jurisdictions. Their negative impact depends on how they are applied and the market characteristics that are affected.

- *Limited access to finance.* Credit to the private sector and deposits remain low, not just when compared to peers at the same income level but also within Latin America. Just one-third of small and medium enterprises have access to loans, and only 12 percent of microenterprises receive finance. Moreover, just 32 percent of small and medium enterprises need to invest but cannot because of financial constraints.

- *Policy-driven distortions that increase the size of the informal sector.* Because social security in Mexico is primarily financed through wage-based contributions, it acts as a tax on salaried employment. This incentivizes firms to move toward nonsalaried contracts, and the illegal evasion of social security, which has negative consequences on productivity and growth. Settling labor disputes based on formal employment contracts is also a long and expensive process.

Bangladesh: How a Shock in Textiles and Apparel Spreads through Local Communities and across the Economy

In the 1990s, Bangladesh took major steps to liberalize international trade. These included (a) cutting the maximum import duty from 350 percent in 1993 to 25 percent in 2005, (b) reducing the number of tariff bands from 15 in 1993 to 4 in 2016, and (c) lowering the unweighted average tariff rate from 70.0 percent in 1992 to 12.3 percent in 2008. Together with other measures aimed at reducing the cost of imported inputs and spurring exports, Bangladesh's liberalization reforms opened the economy to the world. Exports shot up by 2,000 percent between 1990 and 2016, the highest increase in the region, and imports (primarily industrial raw material and capital machinery) rose from close to US$4 million to slightly over US$40 million. Most of these exports were destined for two markets: Europe (59 percent) and the United States (23 percent).

A key question at the center of the current debate about the effects of globalization on welfare is whether the gains from trade remain localized or if they spread through the economy. The study "Short and Long-Run Labor Market Effects of Developing Country Exports: Evidence from Bangladesh" by Robertson et al. (2020) is part of a new body of work that focuses on the export-related impacts of trade reforms in developing countries, rather than the impact on import-competing industries, especially at the local level. Bangladesh is a good example for a number of reasons.

- Since the 2013 Rana Plaza collapse, Bangladesh has been at the center of the debate about the unintended effects of developing country export growth.

- Between 1980 and 2000, it experienced a fundamental reorientation of its economy, becoming far more open.

- Geographic wage dispersion, which gives a snapshot of local labor market integration, is lower than in other countries, such as India.

- Its export growth was highly concentrated within the ready-made garments sector, making its export portfolio far less diversified than those of its neighbors and other comparator countries (figure 3.2), which means that the export shock more closely resembles the assumptions in economic theory.

The study assesses the impact of Bangladesh's export growth on different groups and over time. It also tests whether the informal economy is a short-term adjustment mechanism in Bangladesh following an export shock, as is the case in other countries. The study uses external import demand to capture Bangladesh's export growth. The results illustrate significant impacts through the wage and informal employment channel at the local level in the short term, which spread through the economy over time.

Wages. Subdistricts more exposed to the export shock experienced a Tk 3,062 increase in average annual wages in the short term (2005 to 2010) relative to

FIGURE 3.2 Textiles and Apparel Dominate in Bangladesh
Sectoral breakdown of exports from South Asia and other developing countries, 2016

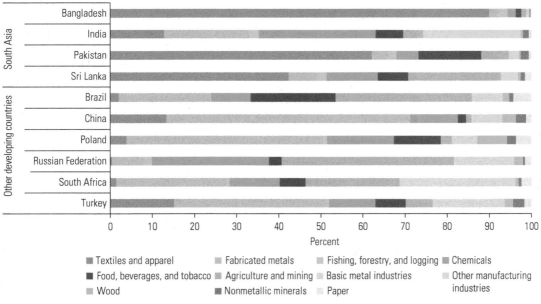

Source: Artuç, Lee, and Bastos 2019.

The Distributional Impacts of Trade

less-exposed subdistricts. These effects spread throughout the economy over time. Although the wage effect was significant between 2005 and 2013, the magnitude of the effect decreased substantially to Tk 658. By 2016, the higher wage effect completely diminished in magnitude and became insignificant in subdistricts more exposed to the export shock (figure 3.3).

Informality. Similarly, informality decreased not only in magnitude but also in statistical significance when taking into consideration additional years. Between 2005 and 2013, informality decreased 0.4 percent, and, between 2005 and 2016, effects on decreasing informality in subdistricts more exposed to export shocks disappeared. A US$100 gain in exports per worker between 2005 and 2010 led to a 0.7 percent decrease in informality in subdistricts with a higher degree of exposure to trade (figure 3.4).

Heterogenous impacts across groups. Consistent with findings in Artuç, Lee, and Bastos (2019) for India, better-off groups had the largest wage gains from trade in Bangladesh. Average wages for high-skilled workers, for instance, increased five times more than the wages of low-skilled workers, and the wages of experienced workers grew twice as much as wages of younger workers. Interestingly, workers in rural areas benefited more in the long term even though wages increased only for urban workers

FIGURE 3.3   Higher Exports Go Hand in Hand with Higher Wages
Change in the average annual real wage after a US$100 increase in exports per worker

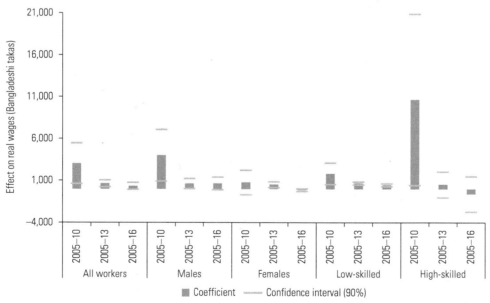

Source: Robertson et al. 2020.
Note: The confidence intervals are set at the 90 percent level. This graph is based on two-stage least squares regression computed to estimate the effect of an increase in exports on real wages and informality. This relationship is estimated for different worker types (male, female, rural, skilled, unskilled, young, and old).

FIGURE 3.4   Higher Exports Go Hand in Hand with Lower Informality

Change in the informality rate after a US$100 increase in exports per worker

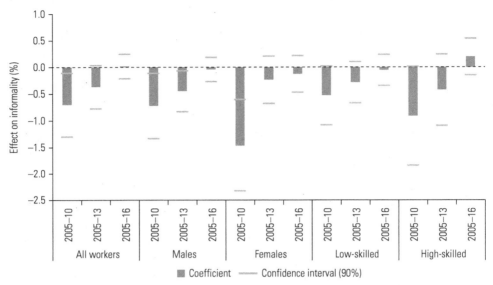

Source: Robertson et al. 2020.

Note: The confidence intervals are set at the 90 percent level. This graph is based on two-stage least squares regression computed to estimate the effect of an increase in exports on real wages and informality. This relationship is estimated for different worker types (male, female, rural, skilled, unskilled, young, and old).

in the short term. Women benefit more than men from trade in terms of its effects on reducing informality (1.5 versus 0.7 percent).

Overall, the study suggests that Bangladesh's labor market outcomes following an export shock differ by region only temporarily. This may be due to the fact that workers are mobile and barriers to migration are relatively low. Like in most countries, wage differentials exist across districts in Bangladesh, but the dispersion of wages decreased consistently between 2005 and 2016, indicating that local labor markets may have become more integrated over time. This finding holds for every year and type of worker. As such, the within-country labor market integration necessary for spreading gains in wages and informality is much higher in Bangladesh than in India, which may explain the differences between these results and those of comparable studies on India.

In addition, the results highlight the importance of ensuring that women can participate in export industries. Rising exports draw women out of informality and into the formal sector. In addition, greater garment exports reduce the wage gap between men and women in the long run, not just in the garment industry but throughout the entire economy, which reflects higher employment rates for women in the garment industry than in most other industries.

The fact that the benefits of trade spread through the economy quickly suggests that factories in poorer and smaller countries such as Bangladesh may have lower adjustment costs, and workers may have greater motivation to be mobile (lower reservation wages). Another factor could be the sector-specific nature of the shock, which may allow workers to be more mobile across sectors in contrast to countries with more diversified economies and thus higher mobility costs and a greater need for emphasizing skills training for workers. In sum, the case of Bangladesh shows that trade remains an important driver of economic development that extends beyond firms and workers in export industries. It also highlights the need to better understand the nature of trade shocks to be able to fully reap the benefits, more carefully design policies that affect employment conditions, and ensure that the effects of trade are inclusive and economy-wide for workers and firms in the long term.

South Africa: How Apartheid's Legacy Shapes the Impact of Trade Liberalization on Local Communities

In the aftermath of the 1994 democratic elections, all homelands—territories reserved for black communities—were legally reintegrated into South Africa. In addition to significant institutional reforms to undo the structure of apartheid that marginalized racial groups, the 1994 democratic election led to an important shift in trade policy from export promotion with import controls to greater openness through liberalization. The newly elected government adopted an ambitious program of tariff liberalization as part of the Uruguay Round, and concluded free trade agreements with the European Union and the Southern Africa Development Community. The number of tariff lines fell from over 12,000 at the beginning of the 1990s to 6,420 in 2006 (Edwards et al. 2009). Figure 3.5 shows that the reduction in effectively applied tariffs was especially important in the manufacturing sector between 1990 and 2006.

What were the medium-term to long-term effects on local labor markets of the sharp tariff reductions observed after the introduction of democracy? The case study "Long-Run Effects of Trade Liberalization on Local Labor Markets: Evidence from South Africa" by Bastos and Santos (forthcoming) draws on municipal-level data from South Africa for the period 1996–2011. Although homelands no longer exist, the study finds that differentials in welfare outcomes still correspond to the geographical areas that constituted the former homelands. Local labor markets more exposed to tariff cuts experienced slower growth in employment and income per capita, with effects increasing over time.

Among municipalities, long-term adverse effects were stronger in those municipalities that included the former homelands and a higher share of the black population. Between 1996 and 2011, a 10 percent reduction in employment-weighted tariffs led to a fall in income per capita of 1.4 percent outside the former homelands, whereas it led to a 3.7 percent reduction in income per capita in municipalities that included at least one former homeland. This may reflect that the former homelands had little economic activity beyond subsistence agriculture so workers whose jobs were affected

FIGURE 3.5 Manufacturing Saw a Prominent Drop in Tariff Rates
Trade liberalization in South Africa

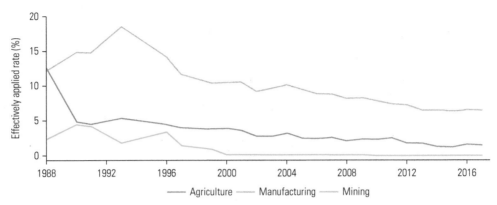

Source: Bastos and Santos, forthcoming.

by the tariff cuts had few economic alternatives to compensate for lost income. Further, these areas were already characterized by highly depressed incomes. If on top of this a municipality that was part of a former homeland was hit by a trade shock in another sector (like manufacturing), it had greater difficulties providing viable outside options for workers displaced by these trade shocks.

Were the impacts on the homelands typical for the South African liberalization experience? The evidence points to overall gains in export growth and diversification. Edwards and Lawrence (2006) find that trade liberalization in the 1990s led to a faster growth of imports and reduced input costs, and that the relative profitability of domestic sales led to higher exports. As a result of liberalization, noncommodity manufacturing exports grew at a faster rate than noncommodity manufacturing imports. Other benefits included access to inputs at world prices, along with a more competitive real exchange rate. Furthermore, the poor benefited from these tariff reductions (Daniels and Edwards 2006). Between 1995 and 2000, the changes to the tariff incidence benefited only the poorest decile; between 2000 and 2004, the bias favored the poor in general. Thurlow (2006) points out that liberalization did not increase poverty and accelerated growth. Liberalization, however, did change the production patterns in favor of rising capital and skill intensity of production, leading to rising inequality and small gains in poverty reduction.

By contrast, later studies find that, although the initial effects from the 1990s reforms were generally quite positive, the overall impact on South Africa to date has been dominated by the China effect in the early 2000s. Declines in production and employment at the aggregate level resulted from rising Chinese imports. Analyzing the data over 1992–2010, Edwards and Jenkins (2013) find that increased import penetration from

China caused South African manufacturing output to be 5 percent lower in 2010 and employment 8 percent lower than they otherwise would have been, as Chinese imports displaced output in labor-intensive sectors.

Similar to Bastos and Santos' findings, Erten, Leight, and Tregenna (2019) find that workers in districts facing larger tariff cuts experienced declines in formal and informal employment in the tradable sector (mostly in manufacturing) relative to districts less affected by cuts. Displaced workers did not find jobs in expanding sectors. They were instead more likely to exit the labor force or access government transfers. Although resulting in aggregate gains, trade liberalization reduced jobs in certain manufacturing sectors, while labor market rigidities and other constraints prevented workers from finding jobs in emerging sectors. The authors attribute this to the unusual features of the South African labor market such as the high base level of unemployment, the small informal sector, high barriers to entry, rigid wages, and an underdeveloped manufacturing sector before liberalization.

What policies could be adopted to address the localized negative impacts of tariff liberalization? Certainly, facilitating geographical labor mobility across sectors, regions, and occupations could be key when mobility is lower. This could be done with well-designed and targeted active labor market policies such as job search assistance and training. Other place-based policies may help revitalize areas depressed by trade shocks and strengthen regional cohesion.

Brazil: How Trade Shocks Affect Wages and Job Opportunities across Regions and Industries

How do trade shocks affect workers? Answering this question requires an understanding of how trade shocks affect workers' wages and the job options they can choose from. This is especially relevant in a country like Brazil, which has gone through major periods of trade liberalization reforms in the 1990s and 2000s and recently experienced sizable swings in external demand. We know from a large body of evidence that Brazil's adjustment to a sharp rise in import competition has been painful, causing declines in wages and employment over time for microregions more exposed to import competition relative to others, along with substantial moving costs.

Dynamic models of trade-induced labor mobility have explored wage differentials and idiosyncratic utility as drivers of mobility across sectors, regions, and occupations. One country case study—"Trade, Jobs, and Worker Welfare" by Artuç, Bastos, and Lee (2019)—breaks new ground by emphasizing an additional motive of mobility: the number of job opportunities provided by different sectors and regions. This new channel matters for workers for two key reasons.

- If a worker can choose a job from a larger pool of opportunities, the best one will probably deliver better welfare outcomes.

- It is more likely that a worker, even when hit by future negative labor demand shocks, will be able to find another job without having to move to a different region or sector.

This new channel is important because there is overwhelming evidence from both developed and developing countries that negative shocks from greater import competition affect wages and employment according to region of residence. However, there is no fully tractable economic model to account for the number of jobs in one or more regions. Additionally, little is known about what happens when there is a positive shock from higher exports.

In this study, the authors introduce a new framework to quantify the impacts of trade shocks on labor mobility and economic benefits to workers, combining the advantages of different methodologies in the literature. The model delivers simple equations that can be used to test the model and estimate parameters. It is then possible to incorporate the model parameters into simulations to analyze the impact of various policy alternatives. The analysis is thus both backward- and forward-looking.

The framework features various drivers of labor mobility across sectors and regions, and it identifies how trade shocks affect those determinants endogenously. The empirical analysis draws on rich employer-employee panel data combined with customs records on Brazil's export transactions during 2003–15. The study first investigates the causal effects of export shocks on labor markets and then conducts three policy experiments to test the importance of labor friction costs and the importance of the job channel.

The study shows the following results.

Higher exports boost employment, wages, and job turnover. A 10 percent increase in exports leads to a 2.3 percent increase in employment and a 3.1 percent increase in average wages. It also leads to fewer workers leaving the region's labor market, more workers entering the region's labor market, and more workers switching occupations or establishments within the region's labor market. In other words, there is more internal "churn" within the labor market.

Moving costs between regions are large compared to moving costs between industries. The average moving cost between sectors is equivalent to a one-time loss of about 64 percent of the annual wage, which is also consistent with the estimates of Dix-Carneiro (2014). The moving cost between regions, though, is equivalent to a one-time loss of about 282 percent of the annual wage.

Higher exports benefit all workers. If both tariffs and transportation costs declined to 30 percent, the welfare increase of an average worker would be equivalent to a permanent 4 percent increase in real wages. The magnitude of gains depends on a worker's industry, though, as well as the region he or she lives in. The average increase in wages, for example, would be about 5 percent for manufacturing workers and more than 6 percent for manufacturing workers in regions with significant export concentration. The average real wage increase for agriculture workers would be about 3.75 percent, significantly smaller than that for most manufacturing workers (figure 3.6).

Higher exports increase the number of jobs on average. The counterfactual decrease in manufacturing trade costs increases the number of jobs by about 6 percent on average, but the change in the number of jobs varies across microregions and sectors. The number of jobs increases in the manufacturing sector in all microregions, whereas the number of jobs declines in the agriculture sector in all microregions (figure 3.7).

Higher exports increase the number of workers in formal employment. The counterfactual decrease in manufacturing trade costs boosts the number of workers in formal employment by about 3.4 percent (figure 3.8). Employment growth in the manufacturing and services sectors accounts for this increase.

Workers in remote regions gain less than others. Agricultural workers in remote regions benefit significantly less from the positive export shocks compared to workers who have access to manufacturing jobs in their own or neighboring regions. Geography determines trade gains for workers.

Overall, these results show that increasing exports has significant and varied effects on the welfare of workers. A decrease in export costs in the manufacturing sector

FIGURE 3.6   A Worker's Industry Matters for Wage Gains
Distribution of gains from trade

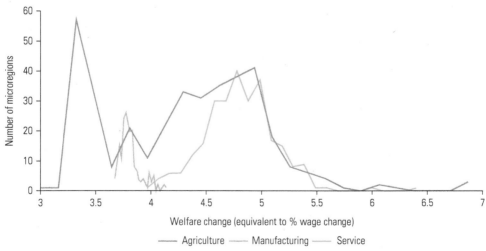

Source: Original calculations based on Artuç, Bastos, and Lee 2019.
Note: The histogram shows the number of microregion-sector pairs on the *y* axis and the change in welfare on the *x* axis.

Manufacturing Sees Biggest Increase in Jobs Compared with Other Sectors
Distribution of change in number of jobs

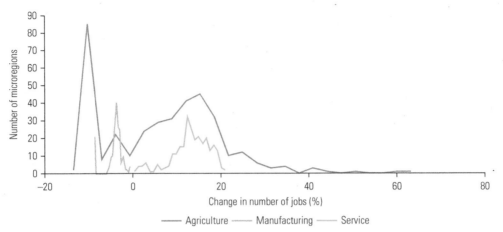

Source: Original calculations based on Artuç, Bastos, and Lee 2019.
Note: Histogram shows the number of microregion-sector pairs on the *y* axis with the percent of job change indicated on the *x* axis.

FIGURE 3.8   A Permanent Increase in Formal Employment

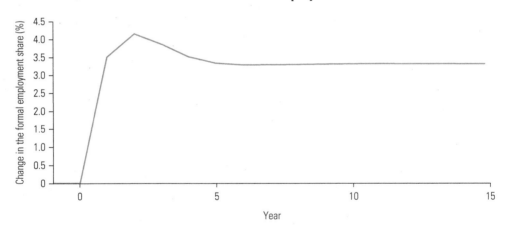

Source: Original calculations are based on Artuç, Bastos, and Lee 2019.
Note: The share is defined by the number of workers in formal industries divided by the working-age population.

affects all workers, irrespective of their original sector. After the positive shock, the manufacturing sector attracts workers from other industries within the same microregion because of the large moving costs between microregions. Workers in remote regions benefit less from this positive shock compared to workers in regions with more job opportunities. The optimal labor market policy will thus have to help workers based on both their industry and region. Targeting a specific industry or specific region may be ineffective.

The Distributional Impacts of Trade

Sri Lanka: How Liberalizing Trade Affects Local Employment

Sri Lanka has taken substantial steps to liberalize its trade, but little is knows about how further trade liberalization could affect local labor markets. Over the past two decades, it has introduced several additional taxes on imports, commonly referred to as "paratariffs." The ad hoc introduction of these taxes and frequent revisions to their rates make the import tax structure complex and unpredictable. Although custom duty rates have largely been kept intact and at a lower rate, the introduction of paratariffs reverses previous efforts aimed at further simplifying and lowering import taxes. Although the number of paratariffs has been reduced from four to two over the past decade, the remaining ones—the Ports and Airports Development Levy and the Export Development Import Cess—affect a significant percentage of imports, and in some cases they grant high protection levels to selected products like agricultural and food products.

As Sri Lanka weighs the best way to further integrate its economy, it is important to understand how the impacts of trade reforms would be distributed at the local level, because there will be winners and losers. One study—"Ex Ante Evaluation of Subnational Labor Market Impacts of Trade Reforms" by Maliszewska, Osorio-Rodarte, and Gupta (2020)—tries to inform the debate by analyzing the impacts of several trade policy changes on subnational employment. The full reform scenario includes the following set of policies: (a) a unilateral paratariff liberalization, (b) a stylized free trade agreement with China; (c) a stylized and expanded free trade agreement with India, and (d) implementation of the World Trade Organization Trade Facilitation Agreement.

The methodology combines a computable general equilibrium model linked to a microsimulation in a top-down approach. The macro-micro approach allows consideration of the impacts of trade policy changes on household income (through wages and sector of employment) and consumption (through sectoral price changes). This analysis required the creation of a new data base extending the Gender Disaggregated Labor Database (GDLD)[1] on wages, employment, and worker education to the provincial level. A similar approach can be applied to several other countries, subject to data availability (box 3.1).

The analysis includes 17 sectors and 35 trading partners, and it simulates the impacts of policy changes through 2028. Given that an ex ante evaluation requires the creation of a counterfactual simulation that serves as a comparison, we use a baseline that follows historical trends and assumes a relatively fast growth of GDP per capita at 4.7 percent over the period from 2018 to 2028. It shows employment in agriculture and related sectors shrinking over time across all districts.

As of 2018, the four largest employers by sector were agriculture (25 percent), manufacturing (18 percent), trade and commerce (18 percent), and social services and others (12 percent). Manufacturing and textiles and apparel jobs are concentrated in

Data Needed to Estimate Labor Market Effects of Trade Reforms at the Subnational Level

Analyzing the trade impact on local labor markets requires establishing a link between macro and micro statistics and simulation models. With the rapid expansion of statistical capacity in developing countries, a growing number of household surveys used to monitor poverty and labor outcomes can also provide reliable estimates of labor market outcomes at the subnational level, typically at the province or state level. Poverty and labor market effects can be drawn with confidence using these newer survey instruments. Using household surveys, for instance, the Global Data Lab[a] provides global subnational development indicators.

Ultimately, the level of regional disaggregation at which a household survey can provide good subnational estimates depends on the design of its sampling framework. The variables required to develop this subnational disaggregation and information about the sampling framework are available in harmonized format in the Gender-Disaggregated Labor Database (GDLD)[b] which was constructed using World Bank collections of harmonized household surveys. Most of the surveys include information at the one-digit regional level (state level). Table 3A.1 in annex 3A shows that 71 surveys for developing countries identify regions at the one-digit level, 29 surveys contain variables at the two-digit level, and 13 surveys contain variables at the three-digit level.

It is possible to overcome the limitations of a survey sampling design by complementing the information in household surveys with census and external data using unit-level small area estimation techniques (Nguyen et al. 2018; Lange, Pape, and Putz 2018), the same techniques used to generate poverty maps.

a. For more on the Global Data Lab, see www.globaldatalab.org.
b. For more on the Gender Disaggregated Labor Database, see http://datatopics.worldbank.org/gdld/.

Colombo, Gampaha, and Kalutara in the Western Province; Kurunegala and Puttalam in the Northwestern Province; and Kandy in the Central Province. The level of urbanization is higher in these districts than elsewhere, but trade- and transportation-related jobs are rather evenly spread out by district (except for Colombo and Gampaha, which account for a disproportionately higher share of workers), as are jobs in social services (education, health care, and domestic personnel). Most jobs in agriculture are found in districts outside of the Western, Northwestern, and Central Provinces.

What are the key findings?

GDP and international trade would expand faster with lower trade barriers. Specifically, 10 years after liberalization, GDP would be expected to be about 2.8 percent higher than in the baseline, and exports would be up by 24 percent and imports by almost 19 percent. Thanks to trade facilitation, lower paratariffs and trade costs would lead to lower prices of inputs for producers and lower prices of imports for consumers, stimulating trade, growth, and a reallocation of resources to the most productive sectors. In the full reform scenario, workers would move out of agriculture and toward the textile and apparel sectors (figure 3.9). There would thus be a net increase in employment, compared to a decline under baseline conditions. As a result, trade policy reforms

FIGURE 3.9 Workers Switch from Agriculture to Textiles and Apparel

Aggregate cumulative labor demand effects by sector in 2028 in the full scenario with respect to baseline

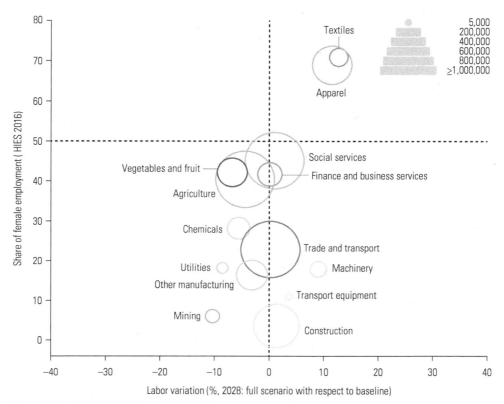

Source: Maliszewska, Osorio-Rodarte, and Gupta 2020.

Note: The communications and electronic equipment sector is excluded. Approximately 98 percent of sectors and workers are represented in HIES 2016. The bubbles represent total estimated workers in each sector. HIES 2016 = Household Income Expenditure Survey 2016.

in this sector can lead to greater value chain integration between local producers of both textiles and apparel and global buyers.

Lower trade barriers would result in lower poverty, greater wage inequality, and higher economic activity in urban areas. Growth helps to alleviate poverty (0.3 percent reduction in the poverty headcount ratio at a purchasing power parity of US$5.50 a day); however, in the full reform scenario, gains in welfare are regressive: the poorest quintile gains 0.8 percent and the richest gains 1.8 percent with respect to the 2028 baseline. The economy expands more rapidly, increasing demand in economic sectors that employ a larger proportion of skilled workers (such as trade and transport, social services, and finance). As a result, wages of skilled workers grow faster than those of nonskilled workers, resulting in higher inequality. Most employment gains are projected in the western regions of Colombo, Gampaha, and Kalutara, where urbanization is highest. The rest of the country would experience a net employment decline (map 3.1).

MAP 3.1 Sri Lanka's Western Urban Areas See the Highest Job Gains

Labor demand changes by district in the full scenario with respect to baseline

Source: Maliszewska, Osorio-Rodarte, and Gupta 2020 based on LINKAGE CGE simulations and HIES 2016.

Note: Green areas experience the highest labor demand, and purple areas the lowest. CGE = Computable General Equilibrium; HIES 2016 = Household Income Expenditure Survey 2016.

Lower trade barriers bring progressive gains in welfare in the short run, but in later years they become regressive. The next step in the study involves running the same scenario of paratariff liberalization using the Household Impacts of Tariffs database and computable general equilibrium–Global Income Distribution Dynamics approach. We find that, in the short term, paratariff liberalization enhances welfare. The effect of price changes benefits the poor: tariff liberalization packages would be associated with gains of

TABLE 3.1 Assessment of Trade Policy Changes on Sri Lankan Welfare

	Ex post analysis using reduced-form methods (local labor market approaches)	Ex ante short-term analysis (HIT)	Ex ante medium- and long-term analysis (CGE-GIDD)
Policy experiment	Impact on wages and informality given an increase in OECD's import demand from Sri Lanka.	Reduction of tariffs and paratariffs as one shock.	Gradual reduction of tariffs and paratariffs over 10 years (same as under the HIT analysis).
Macro impacts	▪ With a US$100 increase in exports per worker, average income would increase by SL Rs 206 between 2002 and 2013. ▪ Export shocks operate primarily through wages rather than employment (average wage increasing by about SL Rs 975 after a US$100 increase in exports per worker).	In the short-term, paratariff liberalization increases economic benefits. The gains are progressive.	▪ Paratariff liberalization could increase Sri Lanka's GDP by 0.8 and 2.0 percent by 2023 and 2028, respectively. ▪ By 2028, exports could grow by 18.3 percent and imports by 9.8 percent. ▪ Key sectors that gain in employment share: textiles, apparel, and other manufacturing. ▪ Output and employment mostly increase in well-established urban regions.
Distributional impacts	▪ The largest impact of exports on wage changes is for high-skilled workers; hence, income inequality between workers increases. ▪ No statistically significant impact of changes in trade on formality of workers.	▪ Paratariff liberalization could confer economic gains of 1.2 percent for the poorest quintile and 0.6 percent for the richest. ▪ The impacts are progressive mostly because the poor are benefiting from lower prices of goods that constitute a large share of their consumption basket. ▪ Income decreases slightly for both poor and rich households, but the impacts are somewhat higher for the richer households.	▪ In the medium to long term, the baseline agricultural sector declines. This process is accelerated in the case of paratariff liberalization. ▪ Growth helps to alleviate poverty (0.3 percent reduction in poverty headcount ratio at a PPP of US$5.50 a day), but increases inequality. ▪ By 2028, the welfare impacts are regressive. Gains are 1.1 percent for the poorest quintile and 1.9 percent for the richest as compared to the baseline. ▪ The regressive impacts are driven by higher wages of skilled workers (rich households), which outweigh the gains for the poor, who mostly benefit from lower prices of goods that constitute a large share of their consumption basket. The sole impact of food prices enhances economic benefits and tilts the gains toward the poor, the poorest quintile gaining 0.7 percent and the richest declining 0.4. percent. As mentioned above, the positive effect of food prices is reversed once the employment and wage effects are taken into consideration.

Source: World Bank.

Note: CGE-GIDD = Computable General Equilibrium–Global Income Distribution Dynamics; HIT = Household Impacts of Tariffs (database); OECD = Organisation for Economic Co-operation and Development; PPP = purchasing power parity; SL Rs = Sri Lanka rupees.

1.20 percent for the poorest quintile and gains of 0.56 percent for the richest, according to the Household Impacts of Tariffs database analysis (see table 3.1). Once the impacts of all adjustments are estimated over the medium and long term, though, the effects become regressive. Even though all households are better off, the gains for the poorest quintile are 1.1 percent but are 1.9 percent for the richest qunitile. The positive consumption effect of lower food prices is outweighed by the income effect, which favors richer households with wage premiums for skilled workers increasing.

What can policy makers do to ensure that the gains from trade are distributed more equally? One way is by upgrading skills for migrant workers, which will benefit both workers and firms. Another is by facilitating better mobility and impoving information and communication technology. A third way is by enforcing progressive labor standards and policies that protect vulnerable workers, especially unskilled migrant women.

Conclusion

The chapter focuses on understanding the distributional impacts of trade in five low- and middle-income countries—Mexico, Bangladesh, South Africa, Brazil, and Sri Lanka—using ex post and ex ante methods. The countries were chosen because they have all undergone significant trade reforms in recent decades (or in the case of Sri Lanka are considering extensive reforms), provide a broad scope of coverage in terms of region and development level, and have high-quality data for econometric analyses of local labor markets. The key findings and lessons are as follows.

- *Mexico.* Increasing exports to richer countries does not necessarily lead to better welfare indicators at the local level. The results show that, although exports have a large and positive impact on total labor incomes, their impact on poverty reduction and per capita household incomes is small. This could be driven by the fact that higher exports lead to a decline in nonlabor income by reducing the volume of remittances. Also, higher exports lead to lower out-migration and higher inflows of return migrants from the United States, leading to a disproportionate increase in unskilled workers at the municipality level, which tends to raise poverty and inequality. By contrast, although exports do not have a significant effect on per capita household incomes, they do affect relative incomes in a progressive way. These findings suggest that, for developing countries to fully reap the benefits of higher integration with rich economies, it is essential to foster stronger links between the tradable and nontradable sectors.
- *Bangladesh.* Trade can be a key driver of development that extends beyond the exporting industries, workers in those industries, or localities where exporting firms cluster. This study finds that wages increase and informality decreases in subdistricts more exposed to Bangladesh's export shock, which is sector-specific and limited predominantly to the female-intensive garment and textile sector. Unlike in other countries, though, these local labor market effects spread quickly.

Over the long run, after higher exports of goods produced by female-dominated workforces, the male-female wage gap closed considerably across the country and not just in apparel. In Bangladesh, which specializes in one specific industry (apparel), the labor market seems to be more integrated compared to larger countries, suggesting that labor adjustment costs could be lower in smaller countries specializing in one sector. Helping Bangladeshi firms increase their exports should thus remain a policy priority.

- *South Africa.* Apartheid-era housing and labor policies created long-lasting barriers to workers' movement across regions, sectors, and occupations. Following its democratic transition in 1994, South Africa introduced substantial and relatively abrupt tariff cuts as part of a broad post-apartheid liberalization process. Although homelands no longer exist, differentials in economic outcomes still mirror the borders of former homelands. Local labor markets more exposed to tariff cuts experienced slower growth in employment and income per capita, the long-term effects on income per capita being stronger than the short-term ones. Facilitating geographical labor mobility may be key when mobility has been historically constrained. Other place-based policies can help revitalize areas negatively affected by trade shocks and strengthen regional cohesion.

- *Brazil.* Increasing exports benefits workers across industries, though the magnitude of gains varies. This study finds that a decrease in export costs in the manufacturing sector affects all workers, irrespective of their original sector. After an increase in exports, the manufacturing sector attracts workers from other industries within the same microregion because of the large costs to move between microregions. Workers in remote regions benefit less from this positive shock compared to workers in urban areas. The optimal labor market policy must thus be both region- and industry-specific.

- *Sri Lanka.* The impact of lower trade barriers would differ both spatially and temporally. This study finds that, if Sri Lanka reduced its trade barriers, there would be a faster expansion of GDP and international trade, as well as less poverty. There would also be greater wage inequality with a concentration of gains in urban areas. It also finds that, in the short term, paratariff liberalization enhances welfare and tilts the effect of price changes toward the poor. Once all adjustments are accounted for in later years, economic effects become regressive even though all households are better off. This is because the positive consumption effect of lower food prices is outweighed by the income effect (which favors richer households with skilled wage premiums increasing). Possible policies to help smooth the transition of workers across regions and sectors include upgrading skills for migrant workers, facilitating better mobility and communication, and enforcing progressive labor standards and policies that protect vulnerable workers.

All of these case studies have significant policy implications. The next chapter focuses on policy responses to mitigate negative distributional impacts related to

Annex 3A: Overview of Gender Disaggregated Labor Database

TABLE 3A.1 Subnational Statistics in Gender Disaggregated Labor Database

Region	Macro regional areas	Surveys with regional variables at the one-digit level	Surveys with regional variables at the two-digit level	Surveys with regional variables at the three-digit level
East Asia and Pacific	7	11	5	4
Europe and Central Asia	4	9	2	0
Latin America and Caribbean	16	13	7	4
Middle East and North Africa	2	5	1	0
South Asia	4	7	2	0
Sub-Saharan Africa	14	26	12	5
Total	47	71	29	13

Source: World Bank.

different types of adjustment costs and maximize the gains from reforms. These include three types of complementary policies that could improve the distributional impacts of trade policy reforms: (a) reducing distortions and strengthening the functioning of markets, (b) reducing trade costs, and (c) speeding up labor market adjustment.

Note

1. For more on the Gender Disaggregated Labor Database, see http://datatopics.worldbank.org/gdld/.

References

Artuç, Erhan, Paulo Bastos, and Eunhee Lee. 2021. "Trade, Jobs, and Worker Welfare." Policy Research Working Paper 9628, World Bank, Washington, DC.

Artuç, Erhan, Robert Cull, Susmita Dasgupta, Roberto Fattal, Deon Filmer, Xavier Gine, Hanan Jacoby, Dean Jolliffe, Hiau Looi Kee, Leora Klapper, Aart Kraay, Norman Loayza, David Mckenzie, Berk Ozler, Vijayendra Rao, Bob Rijkers, Sergio L. Schumkler, Michael Toman, Adam Wagstaff, and Michael Woolcock. 2020. "Toward Successful Development Policies: Insights from Research in Development Economics." Policy Research Working Paper 9133, World Bank, Washington, DC.

Artuç, Erhan, Gladys Lopez-Acevedo, Raymond Robertson, and Daniel Samaan. 2019. *Exports to Jobs: Boosting the Gains from Trade in South Asia.* Washington, DC: World Bank.

Atkin, Dave, and Dave Donaldson. 2015. "Who's Getting Globalized? The Size and Implications of Intranational Trade Costs." Working Paper 21439, National Bureau of Economic Research, Cambridge, MA.

Bastos, Paulo, and Nicolas Santos. Forthcoming. "Long-Run Effects of Trade Liberalization on Local Labor Markets: Evidence from South Africa." World Bank, Washington, DC.

Daniels, Reza, and Lawrence Edwards. 2006. "The Benefit-Incidence of Tariff Liberalisation in South Africa." *Studies in Economics and Econometrics* 31: 69–88.

Dix-Carneiro, Rafael. 2014. "Trade Liberalization and Labor Market Dynamics." *Econometrica* 82 (3): 825–85.

Dix-Carneiro, Rafael, and Brian K. Kovak. 2017. "Trade Liberalization and Regional Dynamics." *American Economic Review* 107 (10): 2908–46.

Edwards, Lawrence, Rashad Cassim, and Dirk Seventer. 2009. "Trade Policy in South Africa." Chapter in *South African Economic Policy under Democracy,* edited by Janine Aron, Brian Kahn, and Geeta Kingdon. Oxford Scholarship Online. 10.1093/acprof:oso/9780199551460.003.0006.

Edwards, Lawrence, and Rhys Jenkins. 2013. "The Impact of Chinese Import Penetration on the South African Manufacturing Sector." *Journal of Development Studies* 51 (4): 447–63.

Edwards, Lawrence, and Robert Lawrence. 2006. "South African Trade Policy Matters: Trade Performance and Trade Policy." Working Paper 12760, National Bureau of Economic Research, Cambridge, MA. https://www.nber.org/system/files/working_papers/w12760/w12760.pdf.

Erten, Bilge, and Jessica Leight. 2019. "Exporting out of Agriculture: The Impact of WTO Accession on Structural Transformation in China." *Review of Economics and Statistics* 1–46. https://direct.mit.edu/rest/article/doi/10.1162/rest_a_00852/97633/Exporting-out-of-Agriculture-The-Impact-of-WTO.

Erten, Bilge, Jessica Leight, and Fiona Tregenna. 2019. "Trade Liberalization and Local Labor Market Adjustment in South Africa." *Journal of International Economics* 118 (C): 448–67.

Lange, Simon, Utz Johann Pape, and Peter Putz. 2018. "Small Area Estimation of Poverty under Structural Change." Policy Research Working Paper 8472, World Bank, Washington, DC.

Maliszewska, Maryla, Israel Osorio-Rodarte, and Rakesh Gupta. 2020. "Ex Ante Evaluation of Subnational Labor Market Impacts of Trade Reforms." Policy Research Working Paper 9478, World Bank, Washington, DC.

McCaig, Brian, and Nina Pavcnik. 2018. "Export Markets and Labor Allocation in a Low-Income Country." *American Economic Review* 108 (7): 1899–941.

Nguyen, Minh Cong, Paul Corral, Joao Pedro Azevedo, and Qinghua Zhao. 2018. "SAE—A Stata Package for Unit Level Small Area Estimation." Policy Research Working Paper 8630, World Bank, Washington, DC.

Robertson, Raymond, Deeksha Kokas, Diego Cardozo, and Gladys Lopez-Acevedo. 2020. "Short and Long-Run Labor Market Effects of Developing Country Exports: Evidence from Bangladesh." Policy Research Working Paper 9176, World Bank, Washington, DC.

Rodriguez-Castelan, Carlos, Emmanuel Vazquez, and Hernan Jorge Winkler. 2020. "Tracing the Local Impacts of Exports on Poverty and Inequality in Mexico." IZA Discussion Paper 13610, IZA Institute of Labor Economics, Bonn, Germany. https://ssrn.com/abstract=3679016.

Thurlow, James. 2006. "Has Trade Liberalization in South Africa Affected Men and Women Differently?" DSGD Discussion Paper 36, International Food Policy Research Institute (IFPRI), Washington, DC.

World Bank. 2019. "Systematic Country Diagnostic: Mexico." Washington, DC: World Bank.

4. Fostering Inclusive Trade: A Policy Agenda

Key Messages

- Expanding trade is a major source of faster growth and employment, and economies that are more open tend to have both higher levels of employment and better-quality jobs. Gains from trade are rarely evenly distributed across the economy, though, and certain regions, industries, firms, and workers can be left worse off following trade reforms. In developing countries, distortions in the economy and in labor markets can mean that reallocating resources after trade liberalization happens only gradually.

- Government policy choices can strongly influence the economic and political impacts of trade reforms. This includes policies that focus on three types of economic objectives: fewer distortions and better functioning markets, lower trade costs, and faster labor market adjustment.

- Maximizing the gains from trade and minimizing negative impacts require a comprehensive and economy-wide approach that focuses on (a) using new data and tools to understand potential distributional impacts ex ante, (b) monitoring implementation, (c) coordinating responses across government, and (d) holding extensive consultations with the private sector and other nongovernmental stakeholders.

- What will it take to establish a global trade policy agenda that delivers for the poor? One key measure should involve building a stronger and more effective multilateral trading system that can counter rising protectionism. Another measure made necessary by recent disasters like the COVID-19 (coronavirus) pandemic and more frequent climate-related shocks would be the urgent need for developing countries to strengthen their policy frameworks and economic foundations for resilient, competitive, and inclusive societies.

Introduction

So far, this report has shown that many developing countries have experienced large aggregate gains from opening up to trade. Expanding trade is a major source of faster growth and employment (Bacchetta and Stolzenburg 2019; Irwin 2019), and economies that are more open tend to have both higher levels of employment and higher-quality jobs (Di Ubaldo and Winters 2020). Although effects are somewhat uneven across countries, the findings from recent research consistently show that the wave of trade reforms in the 1980s and 1990s has had a positive impact on economic growth (Irwin 2019).

Gains from trade are rarely evenly distributed across the economy, though, and certain regions, industries, firms, and workers can be left worse off following trade reforms, particularly in developed countries. As resources move from low- to high-productivity activities, for example, this can be detrimental to industries that were previously profitable thanks to duties on imports that shielded them from foreign competition, making it more expensive for consumers to buy foreign-produced goods (Hoekman and Nelson 2019). In many developing countries, distortions in the economy and in labor markets can mean that the reallocation of resources following trade liberalization happens only gradually. Businesses frequently face barriers to entry and exit, and investors are reluctant to take risks following reforms. This is compounded by inadequate safety nets for facilitating adjustment in many countries, which makes it hard for workers to learn new skills and move to export industries.

The right kind of policy choices can improve both distributional outcomes and the speed of adjustment. Recent work on South Asia highlights the need for targeted policies to support these transitional processes and spread the benefits from trade more widely (Artuç et al. 2019). The importance of such policies has been recognized at the highest levels. The Group of 20 leaders concluded in 2017 that "the benefits of international trade and investment have not been shared widely enough. We need to better enable our people to seize the opportunities and benefits of economic globalization" (G20 Research Group 2017).

The country cases presented in chapter 3 highlight the importance of national policy choices in determining the impact of trade reforms as in the following examples.

- Bangladesh's significant and broad-based benefits from export-led growth arose in part thanks to a relatively integrated labor market with only one major export sector: apparel (Robertson et al. 2020). The country's regional and gender wage inequality has declined over time along with gains from trade also benefiting those working in other sectors.

- Despite export growth in many sectors in South Africa, historically marginalized communities in former homelands have experienced relatively slower growth and benefited less than those living in more dynamic regions (Bastos and Santos, forthcoming). This result was at least partly due to low labor mobility combined with the dual trade shock of liberalization reforms in the 1990s and intense import competition from China after it joined the World Trade Organization (WTO) in 2001.

- The combined impact of high levels of return migration and weak backward linkages from export sectors in Mexico have limited the reduction in poverty from the country's impressive export boom after the North American Free Trade Agreement (NAFTA) went into effect (Rodríguez-Castelán, Vazquez, and Winkler 2020).

These differences reflect how structural features of an economy and the quality of economic policy can affect both the distributional outcomes of trade and the time frame over which these impacts occur.

In recent years, there has been a lot of progress in our understanding of these issues, thanks to empirical advances, many of which are highlighted in chapters 2 and 3. The fact that there are both winners and losers from trade reforms has always been central to trade theory. In recent years, though, our ability to predict outcomes before reforms take place has improved (Autor 2018), despite it being generally more difficult to identify winners than losers (Artuç et al. 2020). The Sri Lanka case study in chapter 3 exemplifies some of these advances (Maliszewska, Osorio-Rodarte, and Gupta 2020). Recent work also highlights that adjustment costs for specific groups can be significant and long-lasting. The rising importance of global value chains (GVCs) has altered these dynamics, changing the demand for skills and contributing to labor market polarization as high-skill workers in advanced and middle-income economies benefit (Lee and Yi 2018; World Bank 2020). At the same time, evidence suggests that technological change may be a bigger driver of these dynamics than trade (Beverelli et al. 2018), as shocks propagate more frequently and unpredictably through GVCs than before (Acemoglu, Ozdaglar, and Tahbaz-Salehi 2015; De Soyres and Gaillard 2019).

When these shocks result from government decisions to initiate reforms unilaterally, bilaterally, or at the regional and multilateral levels, there is greater latitude for policy makers to assess likely distributional outcomes and promote greater awareness of these before reforms are implemented. The 2000 United States–Vietnam Bilateral Free Trade Agreement, for example, which entailed extensive reductions in US tariffs on Vietnamese exports, resulted in positive labor market outcomes in Vietnam (McCaig and Pavcnik 2018). In other cases, countries have been unexpectedly affected by policy choices made elsewhere, as the "China shock" literature on the global impacts of China's entry into the WTO has shown (see box 2.1 in chapter 2).

Furthermore, the economic impacts of trade reforms have political ramifications. The potentially significant redistributive effects of trade policy changes make these processes highly politicized and subject to intense advocacy, lobbying, and, potentially, industry capture (Grossman and Helpman 1994; Rodrik 2018).[1] The perception of concentrated impacts on workers in industries in developed countries negatively affected by import competition has been a significant obstacle to further trade liberalization and has served as an argument for protectionism and more intense economic nationalism (Rodrik 2020), even if these negative distributional impacts are often driven by other causes (Hoekman and Nelson 2019). The fact that trade gains tend to be widely distributed and losses concentrated by region and sector (even if only relatively so) can constrain public support for further trade integration or even cause backsliding on prior commitments (Artuç et al. 2020).

This chapter argues that policy choices made by governments can strongly influence the economic and political impacts of trade reforms. It focuses on three complementary policy aims (our "pillars"): (a) reducing distortions and strengthening the functioning of markets, (b) reducing trade costs, and (c) speeding up labor market adjustment. These policy objectives are highly complementary. The first is critical for enabling the more productive parts of the economy to grow and expanding the benefits arising from new export opportunities and greater market access. The second helps ensure that the export competitiveness of domestic firms is not hampered by excessive costs and unnecessary bureaucracy. The third facilitates the reallocation of workers toward more productive activities to maximize gains from openness to trade and ensure that adjustment costs are borne by society at large rather than by the few workers whose jobs are displaced.

These three pillars draw on different types of policies that jointly address the key sources of high adjustment costs hampering the distribution of the gains from trade throughout the economy and exacerbating transitional unemployment following shocks, as shown in figure 4.1. The nature of the trade shock, regardless of whether it originates from trade policy reforms initiated by a government itself or from those initiated by a different country, is taken as a given, so the focus must remain on complementary policies that improve distributional outcomes.[2] This chapter is structured around these pillars, starting with an exploration of each and concluding with a discussion on how to improve the "nuts and bolts" of pursuing and implementing trade policy reforms at the domestic level, as well as priorities for a global policy agenda that delivers benefits for the poor.

Although chapter 4 draws on lessons from both advanced and developing countries, its focus is on low- and middle-income countries. This is because optimal policy responses depend on economic and political circumstances such as the level of the country's development as well as the structure and complexity of its export basket. The scope and relative effectiveness of policy responses to trade reforms in low-income countries are therefore likely to be quite different. Additionally, the degree of liberalization differs widely: traditionally, agreements involving developing countries primarily focused on lowering trade barriers, whereas more complex agreements seeking to achieve regulatory harmonization are becoming standard for wealthier countries (Mattoo, Rocha, and Ruta 2020). A country's development level and endowments are thus key in making trade policy choices, as are different complementary policies aimed at creating better trade-related outcomes.[3]

Complementary Policy Priorities for Inclusive Trade

Pillar 1: Reduce Distortions and Strengthen the Functioning of Markets

Improve the business environment

There is a strong argument for addressing anticompetitive behavior in the context of trade reforms in order to increase the gains from trade. A recent World Bank report on

FIGURE 4.1 Overview of Complementary Policies

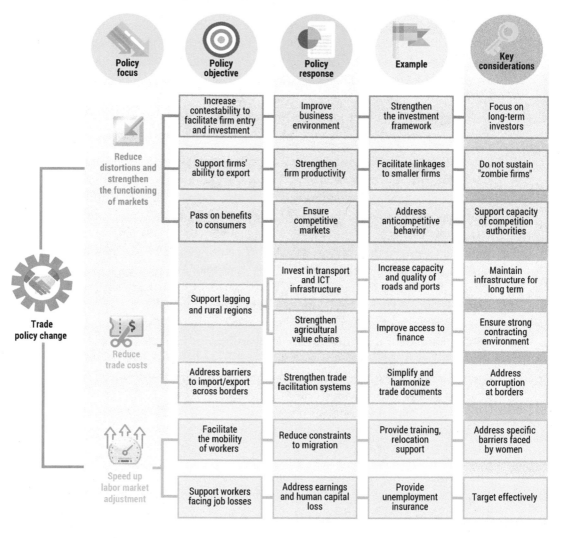

Source: World Bank.

Note: "Zombie firms" are companies that remain in business but are unable to service their debt, making them dependent on continued support from creditors. ICT = information and communication technology.

strengthening Argentina's global integration makes the interdependence between trade, competition, and investment explicit (Martínez Licetti et al. 2018). It proposes an agenda that covers policy reforms in all three areas at both the national and subnational levels to generate mutually reinforcing effects such as increased foreign direct investment (FDI) spillovers, a reduced exercise of market power, and productivity improvements between and within firms and sectors.

In the absence of significant barriers to market contestability and distortions, increased openness to trade results in a reallocation of resources from these sectors to export industries that benefit from the new opportunities to access global markets. These trade-offs are not inevitable, and many times both import-competing and export sectors gain from this process. For example, during a period of major industrialization (1971 to 1991), employment rose in both the export and import sectors in Mauritius despite lower trade barriers creating more competition for the latter (Di Ubaldo and Winters 2020). In Mexico, however, the competition shock from China's entry in the global economy led to a reallocation of market share within firms and between firms, with larger and more productive firms more likely to weather the shock, whereas smaller, less productive firms suffered (Iacovone, Rauch, and Winters 2013).

Another way to improve the business environment is by strengthening the institutions that govern it, because these influence the likelihood of benefits materializing in postreform contexts. This finding goes back to work by Rodriguez and Rodrik (1999), who demonstrate that the impacts of trade policy reforms are sensitive to conditioning factors that vary at the country level. Freund and Bolaky (2008) support this finding by providing evidence that trade leads to higher income in flexible economies where business regulations facilitate firm entry. They find that, in countries that facilitate firm entry, a 1.0 percent increase in trade is associated with a 0.5 percent increase in per-capita income, but trade has no impact on income in more closed economies. Similarly, Chang, Kaltani, and Loayza (2009) show that the impacts of trade liberalization depend on the existence of distortions in nontrade institutions and the feasibility of removing them. The authors find that open trade leads to faster economic growth, but only in countries with a business-friendly environment. A survey by Irwin (2019) of cross-country studies over recent decades concludes that countries that did not experience growth gains after trade reforms often counteracted the reforms by protecting domestic sectors, adopted contractionary macroeconomic policies after reforms, or experienced political instability.

A business environment that is conducive to attracting FDI is especially important for countries hoping to benefit from increased trade openness. Reviewing the period from 1950 to 1998, Wacziarg and Welch (2008) find that 21 percent of the effect of liberalization on growth came from greater capital investment. These impacts were particularly significant for countries that liberalized during the 1980s and 1990s and especially salient in developing countries where the potential for higher domestic investment is constrained, increasing the reliance on foreign investors to bolster productivity gains through the diffusion of knowledge and technology to local workers (Farole and Winkler 2014). Vietnam's experience is emblematic of this. Its growth in recent decades was driven largely by liberalization and large inflows of external purchasing power, enabling it to move from subsistence agriculture to the development of agglomeration economies and industrial development (Ohno 2009).

The importance of the broader business environment in driving a strong investment response to trade reforms is also supported by preferences expressed by investors. A recent global survey of over 750 international business executives involved with the operations of multinational corporations in developing countries highlights numerous country characteristics as being particularly important for investors (Kusek and Silva 2018). In order of importance, these include (a) political stability and security, (b) quality of the legal and regulatory environment, (c) size of the domestic market, and (d) macroeconomic stability and a favorable exchange rate. Although some of these variables are outside of a country's control (such as domestic market size), governments have considerable latitude to design regulations that are simple, transparent, and predictable.

Strengthening investment-related institutions and investment agreements can be conducive to facilitating this process. An important dimension of this includes the strength of institutions to attract investment. Costa Rica, Malaysia, and Morocco have been able to attract transformative investments supporting GVC integration using investment promotion strategies (World Bank 2020). These have included (a) developing FDI investment reform treaties, (b) improving the effectiveness of policies and efforts aimed at attracting and facilitating FDI (such as enhanced investor entry regimes), (c) improving the effectiveness of investment incentives, and (d) strengthening investor confidence by reducing the risk of expropriation and promoting best practices in investment grievance management (Echandi, Krajcovicova, and Qiang 2015; Qiang, Liu, and Steenbergen 2021).

Strengthen the capabilities of firms

There are many ways that governments can help firms to become successful exporters. A key area centers on boosting productivity by strengthening capabilities, improving managerial and organizational practices, innovation competencies, and worker skills (Bloom and van Reenen 2010; McKenzie and Woodruff 2017). This includes, for example, providing consulting services to executives to improve management practices and providing managers and workers with coaching and mentoring (Fafchamps and Quinn 2018). Another way is to increase the adoption of relevant technologies in priority sectors (Cirera and Maloney 2017). In this regard, Atkin et al. (2019) suggest (a) providing financial support to businesses to acquire more technology-intensive equipment, (b) interventions to incentivize technology upgrading through improved information provision or incubator programs, and (c) laws that create an enabling environment for upgrading. Another way is helping firms formalize. Bosch, Goñi-Pacchioni, and Maloney (2012) find that, after trade reforms (1983–2002), higher informality in Brazil was largely driven by domestic reforms that increased firing costs and introduced tighter restrictions on overtime work. Recent research from Brazil (Dix-Carneiro et al. 2021) finds that, although policies to lower informality can boost productivity and welfare, it can come at the expense of some potential increases in unemployment.

There are also many ways in which governments can address capital constraints faced by firms, especially during trade adjustment. This is particularly the case for smaller firms in developing countries (Fafchamps et al. 2014). It can also be the case for larger firms, as evidence from India and Peru shows (Banerjee and Duflo 2014; Paravisini et al. 2015). One way that governments can help is with programs to increase the provision of credit to firms for reorienting business models, finance investment in new technologies, or strengthen sectors that are likely to expand (IMF, World Bank, and WTO 2017). Better access to trade finance through concessional facilities can also be essential to help firms access global markets (World Bank and WTO 2015). Lessons from Tunisia's export-matching grant program, FAMEX, demonstrate that addressing credit constraints preventing firms from exporting is not straightforward. Although FAMEX achieved significant gains in the short term, the impact dissipated after three years (Cadot et al. 2015).

Another way to increase the export response focuses on taking a broad approach to tackling trade restrictions. One of the benefits of trade openness, including for firms producing import-competing products, is access to cheaper foreign inputs. Amiti and Konings (2007) show that, for manufacturing firms in Indonesia, a 10 percent fall in input tariffs led to productivity gains of 12 percent for firms that imported inputs, a result that finds support in numerous advanced economies, as well as in China and India (Amiti et al. 2017; Colantone and Crinò 2014; Topalova and Khandelwal 2011). Furthermore, addressing restrictions on trade in services while addressing tariffs on goods can reduce costs for firms and enable integration into GVCs (OECD 2017; World Bank 2020) because of the centrality of services as inputs into manufacturing.[4]

Governments can also improve both aggregate and distributional gains from trade by supporting the development of linkages from large multinational firms to smaller producers. Indeed, in Mexico (see chapter 3), poor linkages between the tradable and nontradable sectors have limited the positive effects of exports on the growth of firms in nontradable sectors and, thus, income per capita (Rodríguez-Castelán, Vazquez, and Winkler 2020). A recent study on Costa Rica shows that, after domestic firms started supplying multinational firms, they experienced strong, persistent improvements in performance (Alfaro-Ureña, Manelici, and Vásquez 2019). On average, firms increased their workforce by 26 percent and saw gains in standard measures of total factor productivity of 6 to 9 percent after four years. Although the development of linkages is far from automatic (especially in low-income settings), there are many ways to strengthen such linkages, notably by providing information, facilitating business-to-business relationships, and using regulatory approaches (Farole and Winkler 2014). Any kind of more prescriptive rules (like local content requirements) should not be so onerous as to discourage investment, though.

Pass on benefits to consumers

The importance of increasing market contestability is also central to maximizing the gains from trade on the consumption side (see chapter 2). Factor and product market distortions hinder how liberalization reforms are passed through to consumers. These impacts can be significant in the retail sector, which tends to be far less competitive in developing countries than in developed countries (Atkin et al. 2019).

The Distributional Impacts of Trade

One reason for this is that incumbent firms restrict entry into their sectors (Busso and Galiani 2019).

In addition, the high transaction costs in many of these sectors can significantly reduce benefits to the poor. Competition stimulates the willingness of firms to pay higher wages to workers and can reduce the level of informality in an economy (Anand and Khera 2016; Charlot, Malherbet, and Terra 2015). Depetris-Chauvin, Depetris-Chauvin, and Mulangu (2017) find that a lack of competition in transport, distribution, and logistics services means that gains from trade reforms can be quite small for poor households. There is thus a further strong, pro-poor argument for addressing anticompetitive behavior in the context of trade reforms. A key lever is strengthening competition authorities as well as international cooperation on standards to even the playing field (OECD 2017). Possible measures include (a) pro-competition regulations that open markets and remove anticompetitive sectoral regulation, (b) promoting competitive neutrality and nondistortive public state aid, and (c) effective competition law and antitrust enforcement (Dauda 2020).

Pillar 2: Reduce Trade Costs

Invest in connective infrastructure, especially in lagging regions

Reducing trade costs through better infrastructure allows poor households to access markets and move from subsistence farming to cash crops while enabling small and medium enterprises to grow and access internationally competitive inputs and technology. This is supported by historical experiences, such as the finding by Fajgelbaum and Redding (2018) that the railway network in Argentina in the late nineteenth century was instrumental to the country's economic development at the time. In India, the construction of the railroad network decreased trade costs and intraregional price gaps, increased interregional and international trade, and boosted incomes (Donaldson 2018). As such, focusing on persistently high domestic trade costs that constrain remote regions is essential to more widely sharing the benefits from trade liberalization.

This is particularly relevant for supporting lagging and less industrialized regions within countries. Industries often cluster geographically, and, in turn, the impacts of trade shocks are often highly geographically concentrated. Moreover, in addition to geographical distance, crossing a border can add considerable trade frictions that go beyond impediments experienced at borders (such as trade and transport facilitation bottlenecks or even tariffs). Policies that make borders less of a barrier and support the integration and competitiveness of regions and firms that could lose out under reforms can thus have a large impact. Remoteness and poor connective infrastructure raise production costs and can make critical goods and services unavailable. A one-day reduction in domestic trading times could lead to a 7 percent increase in exports, equivalent to a cut of 1.5 percentage points on all importing-country tariffs (Freund and Rocha 2011).

Reducing trade costs also requires having good access to quality seaports and air connectivity. Because 90 percent of trade transits by sea, the quality and accessibility of ports have substantial impacts on global trade patterns, and in turn on the ability of countries to benefit from trade (Atkin et al. 2019; Nordås and Piermartini 2004). For perishable goods such as horticultural products, though, airport connectivity can also be essential for export growth. Campante and Yanagizawa-Drott (2018) show that, once two cities are connected through an air link, there is a substantial increase in proxy measures for integration such as cross-ownership of companies and the number of business events involving the two cities.

Moreover, with the increasing importance of e-commerce, access to the internet is becoming essential to access foreign markets for firms in developing countries. In recent years, cross-border flows of data have surged dramatically while also facilitating the trade of traditional goods, and electronic commerce platforms have reduced trade costs by as much as 60 percent (World Bank 2021). This has only become more salient during the COVID-19 pandemic with social distancing restrictions greatly increasing demand for online trade. Improvements in information and communication technology (ICT) connectivity including liberalizing ICT services, investing in ICT infrastructure, and expanding high-speed broadband are now essential. They allow small firms that often employ more low-skill and informal workers to compete more efficiently abroad. In China, the dramatic export expansion over the past two decades was greatly facilitated by the rollout of the internet across provinces. Firms were able to increase exports, production, and employment, particularly thanks to lower information costs for buyers and input suppliers (Fernandes, Ferro, and Wilson 2019).

Support to agricultural value chains can be another way of strengthening regions affected by trade adjustment, especially because investment in rural infrastructure is often not enough. Focusing on agricultural and agroprocessing value chains can often cover a broad set of market failures simultaneously, including access to finance, lack of modern technology, and a lack of marketing capacities and management skills, which in turn helps absorb poor and low-skill workers (World Bank 2020). A key issue, in this regard, is ensuring a strong contracting environment along the value chain to ensure, for example, that contracted farmers do not pass on technology to those outside the chain and that transparent pricing mechanisms are established (Fuglie et al. 2019).

Strengthen trade facilitation and trade-related institutions

Reducing costs that firms face at the border can also make a difference. Trade facilitation initiatives in particular can help countries reduce the time and cost for cross-border trade by streamlining the technical and legal procedures and processes for products moving across borders.[5] Removing administrative and regulatory bottlenecks at borders can have powerful effects on lowering trade costs, enhancing competitiveness, and supporting economic development. In many developing countries, customs and border delays are now a bigger impediment to trade than tariffs. A recent analysis finds that the most significant economic benefits from the implementation of the African Continental Free Trade Area would come from the reduction in nontariff barriers and from trade facilitation measures (World Bank 2020a). This is particularly relevant to addressing many of the potential impacts of the COVID-19 pandemic because trade facilitation is integral to the movement of medical goods and other related medical equipment including vaccines.

Another way to lower trade costs is by addressing barriers to trade across borders. A key obstacle is the prevalence of inefficient procedures, corruption, harassment, and tariff evasion at the border, which tend to be most harmful for smaller firms and women traders. Such barriers can have significant impacts on how firms organize their production and trade, and in extreme cases can result in firms taking on considerable additional costs to avoid the uncertainty associated with paying bribes (Sequiera and Djankov 2014). There are, however, institutional and technological solutions. In Madagascar, providing better information to customs inspectors and monitoring through third-party inspections has markedly improved detection (Chalendard et al. 2020).

There is also a need for complementary policies that strengthen institutions related to trade and investment. These can include measures to strengthen export promotion bodies to address information failures on the buyer side, where knowledge about trade partners might be constrained. In this regard, the focus should be less about promoting individual firms and more about reducing coordination failures linked to information frictions and to developing tools such as web platforms that list available exporters (Atkin et al. 2019).

Regulatory harmonization on issues like standards can also increase gains from trade. Disdier, Fontagné, and Cadot (2015) find that a north-south harmonization of technical barriers to trade (one category of nontariff measures) expands trade between developed and developing countries. Czubala, Shepherd, and Wilson (2009) find that nonharmonized standards reduce African exports of textiles and clothing to the European Union, and they suggest that efforts to promote African exports of manufactures may need to be complemented by measures to reduce the cost impacts of product standards, including international harmonization. Most recently, Fernandes et al. (2019) similarly show that product standards significantly affect foreign market access for firms.

Pillar 3: Speed Up Labor Market Adjustment

Facilitate the mobility of workers

Policies that help workers move to growing export industries and regions are essential to increase the benefits from trade. Generally, some losses from trade-related adjustment are inevitable, and a central lesson from past experiences of trade reforms is the importance of ensuring that workers can move to new jobs as rapidly as possible (Cirera, Willenbockel, and Lakshman 2014; Hollweg et al. 2014). This includes helping workers shoulder costs connected with finding a new job (such as the cost of searching). The costs for workers to relocate tend to be relatively higher in poorer countries (Artuç, Lederman, and Porto 2015). In the absence of support, sectoral reallocation frequently proceeds very slowly, and many displaced workers end up in the informal economy.

There are often substantial barriers to free movement of workers across a country. These include a lack of information about the returns to migration as well as frictions in land markets and financial markets (Lagakos 2020). Munshi and Rosenzweig (2016), for example, show that improving insurance markets would lead to substantial reductions in the misallocation of rural workers, in particular those currently residing in rural areas, because they lack formal insurance and depend on informal communal risk-sharing arrangements.

Deliberate labor policies and laws that prevent firms from hiring additional workers and incentivize smaller firm sizes make moving across regions more difficult (Lopez-Acevedo, Medvedev, and Palmade 2017). In China, migration frictions caused by its household registration system (*hukou*) create a significant barrier to better geographical allocation of labor (see also chapter 2). Zi (2016) finds that abolition of the *hukou* system would increase gains from tariff reductions by 2 percent and alleviate negative distributional consequences. Furthermore, frictions in land markets linked to inheritance systems can also create barriers. In India, research shows that, if land markets are highly distorted, inheriting land can act as a barrier to exiting agriculture and migrating to urban areas even though this would increase an individual's wealth (Fernando 2020). In these cases, land market reforms (like the computerization of land registries and changes to inheritance laws) can facilitate labor mobility and increase agricultural productivity, enabling more productive farmers to work in the sector. Although politically more challenging, improving labor mobility across borders would have even greater impacts (Clemens 2011; Sáez 2013).

Many of these obstacles are particularly significant for women. Women tend to make up a larger part of the labor force in trading firms than in nontrading firms and have been large beneficiaries of export booms in many developing countries (World Bank and WTO 2020). In many countries, though, women continue to face gender-specific challenges in labor markets. In order to support the integration of women in the labor market, providing childcare and training programs and addressing legal barriers to labor market participation are central priorities (World Bank 2019). Similarly, programs that help women from poorer regions move to cities for training and employment in export sectors have had significant positive results in Bangladesh (World Bank 2017).

Direct moving subsidies are one example of such a policy to offset moving costs. Lake and Millimet (2016), for example, find that a full subsidy covering 100 percent of mobility costs almost completely compensates the displaced worker's aggregate losses. Another possibility is allowing the portability of social welfare benefits across state borders to aid the mobility of workers, which India is gradually implementing across participating states through public distribution system ration cards. These provide subsidized food to low-income households and serve as the proof of identity for a wide range of social protection schemes and public services. Drawing on evidence from Indonesia, Cali, Hidayat, and Hollweg (2019) also argue that, in addition to policies that lower housing prices through increased supply, a more direct way to reduce transitional unemployment from a labor market shock is through housing benefits that reduce labor mobility costs.

As discussed in chapter 2, trade reforms often affect informal sector employment and welfare differently than employment in formal sector firms. As such, it is important to better integrate our understanding of how to support informal sector workers in the context of trade shocks. This has a few implications (Qiang and Kuo 2020). First, there may be value in de-linking support to firms and full formalization. Providing access to adjustment programs to informal firms by, for example, creating partial registration mechanisms is also valuable. Second, partnering with nongovernmental organizations and business associations can help represent the interests of informal sector firms while interventions targeting clusters of firms rather than individual businesses can generate market linkages and productivity spillovers. Governments can make support conditional on this being based on both formal and informal supply chain partners.

Training programs and investments in skills can greatly improve the ability of formal and informal sector workers—especially the younger ones—to move to new jobs. This can be done through subsidies and tax benefits that encourage investments by firms in training. The Republic of Korea's levy rebate system sets aside a portion of payroll tax with employers as a training fund that subsequently provides reimbursements if employers offer this training (Artuç et al. 2019). The effects of training programs, however, can vary greatly. Three main factors are linked to a program's success: targeting, intensity, and environment. Investing in education at all levels (that is, beyond just the training programs) is essential to ensure that workers can adapt to evolving labor market demands, whether these are caused by trade or technological change. Ibarrarán and Rosas-Shady (2009) find that the effects of training programs also vary according to certain demographic and regional characteristics. Macroeconomic context has played a central role in determining the gains from training programs because most of these programs in developing countries do not tackle the roots of unemployment and rely on low investments and the expectation of high returns. Even though they are mostly cost-effective and help increase participant employability, larger labor market strategies are needed to accompany these programs. There is significant scope to expand such programs, especially for informal sectors.

Take the cases of Turkey and Peru

In Turkey, the National Employment Agency has considerably increased access to training programs as a means to mitigate the spike in unemployment following the 2009 global recession. An evaluation by Hirshleifer et al. (2016) finds a modest positive impact on employment outcomes through the courses provided by public institutions but a significant impact from those offered by private providers. Reasons why the public program did not do better include high dropout rates and shortfalls in course quality and length.

In Peru, the Projoven program, which ran from 1996 until 2010, aimed to facilitate access to the formal labor market for young people with limited resources. It did so by providing short-term classroom technical training, later supplemented with a three-month professional internship financed by companies themselves, which incentivized firms to commit to future work. An evaluation by Díaz and Rosas-Shady (2016) suggests that the program increased opportunities for finding a formal job in an economic context typified by high labor informality.

Support workers facing job loss

Another group of policies centers on adjustment assistance and active labor market programs. Economic adjustment is not trade-specific, and most often results from innovation and technological progress. Successful programs to support labor market adjustments, then, focus on facilitating reallocation and supporting displaced workers independently of the cause.

There are programs, particularly in advanced countries, that combine addressing labor market rigidities with financial support to workers who lose their jobs. Denmark's "flexicurity" model has relatively few restrictions to hiring and firing workers but provides significant investment in active labor market programs to enhance the employability of workers and connect them to jobs while also maintaining a broad-based unemployment benefit system (Bacchetta, Milet, and Monteiro 2019; World Bank 2019). There is an increasing focus on targeting incentive programs such as tax credits or wage subsidies directly to lagging regions, though such measures will have long-term success only if they are combined with broader regional development policies to improve the competitiveness of the local economy (World Bank 2020).

Developing countries have less fiscal and institutional capacity to support targeted labor market programs. As a result, most of them rely on social security nets and labor market programs that are not population-specific. China and Vietnam can apply their comprehensive unemployment insurance schemes to help laid-off workers, and China now has a targeted trade adjustment system. India, by contrast, uses public information technology colleges to address shortages of skilled workers. Latin America offers general assistance to help firms boost productivity and competitiveness or maintain employment (see box 4.1).

The impact of labor market programs to support adjustment has been mixed. Whereas job search programs are often effective in the short term, training programs have larger long-term impacts (Card, Kluve, and Weber 2018). Moreover, Card, Kluve,

Active Labor Market Policies and Programs in Developing Countries and Their Impacts

In Latin America, most labor market programs are not trade-specific. They instead offer general assistance that can help eligible firms boost their productivity and competitiveness or maintain their employment levels. Overall, the programs tend to be effective at supporting displaced workers. In Mexico, the PROCAMPO program was established in 1993 to compensate for expected price declines in crops after the initiation of the North American Free Trade Agreement (NAFTA). It provided farmers with cash transfers and covered 90 percent of Mexico's cultivated area (Lederman, Lopez-Acevedo, and Savchenko 2014).

In Vietnam, the unemployment insurance program was established after the financial crisis of 2008 and later expanded to cover most workers in the formal economy (Cutler and Bell 2018). To receive benefits, workers had to have been laid off from a firm experiencing a business downturn or a natural disaster. Although benefits include a basic salary, childcare bonuses, job search allowances, and job training, coverage is limited, given Vietnam's large informal economy. Over the years, a growing number of workers have claimed the unemployment insurance. At least one study finds that the reemployment rate is not high. A major opportunity area for the government is to improve the quality of and access to training because less than 5 percent of all people receiving the unemployment allowance receive vocational training (Ngo 2016).

In China, a universal unemployment insurance scheme was established in 1986 to protect displaced workers from the large-scale privatization of many state-owned enterprises. The program was later expanded to include private firms and other public firms, farmers, and, recently, migrant workers (Cutler and Bell 2018). The goal was to encourage further migration from rural areas to cities, and this worked. The benefits include unemployment insurance payments, medical subsidies, coverage of daily expenses, and possible job training to improve employment qualifications and help workers find reemployment (Lee 2000). Coverage, however, is narrow, and the program has a weak role in promoting reemployment and preventing or stabilizing unemployment (ILO 2013). In addition, a trade adjustment program for firms was launched in 2017 in the Shanghai Pilot Free Trade Zone. Its objective is to provide trade adjustment assistance (TAA) for firms experiencing losses as a result of trade frictions, following the rationale of TAA in other countries. TAA includes consulting, employee training, export credit insurance, and supply chain and risk management for two years. Given the TAA program's recent implementation, its efficacy on helping firms is still uncertain.

In India, the information technology (IT) boom of the 1990s and 2000s resulted in a shortage of skilled workers, causing the Indian government to establish public IT colleges in less-developed areas that also struggled to attract private IT colleges. Ghose (2019) reviews the impact of this intervention and finds that it increased the supply of workers with IT skills, provided educational opportunities to less-favored communities, and helped reduce income inequalities.

In Africa, the literature on adjustment programs is more limited, but a recent World Trade Organization volume, *Making Globalization More Inclusive* (Bacchetta, Milet, and Monteiro 2019) offers evidence from Morocco. Belghazi and Berbich (2019) review labor market adjustment policies adopted in response to the 2008 financial crisis to support jobs in the textile, clothing, leather, and footwear industries. They find that only a small number of firms and workers benefited from the scheme and that it failed to address key competitive risks by firms, including competition from smuggling and informal sector firms, as well as the declining attractiveness of the sector to younger workers.

and Weber (2018) find that impacts tend to be larger during a recession. Training also affects women more than men, as well as participants who are returning from long-term unemployment. McKenzie (2017) finds only a modest impact, especially given the high cost of these programs,[6] but Escudero et al. (2019) find that, in Latin America, these programs have been especially effective at increasing employment (including formal employment). It is nonetheless important to recognize that, even with the best policy responses in place, there are likely to be many who permanently lose from trade adjustment. For these groups, safety net measures may be the only possible response.

Implementing a Policy Agenda for Inclusive Trade

Address Distributional Impacts through Preparation, Sequencing, and Consultation

Understand potential distributional impacts ex ante
On top of the complementary policies that governments employ to maximize gains from trade and ensure better distributional outcomes, there is significant scope to address many of these issues before undertaking reforms. In recent years, there have been big improvements in the availability of microdata and in computing power, and a growing number of real-time data sources (see chapter 2). Furthermore, a better understanding of the firm structure within value chains and production networks has improved our ability to predict how the impact of shocks (whether related to trade policy or other sources) is likely to propagate across borders, sectors, and population groups (Carvalho and Tahbaz-Salehi 2019; Huneeus 2018). Additionally, the availability of highly granular geospatial data enables analysis of the subnational distribution of economic activity at a very fine geographical scale. Increasingly precise big data sources from cell phones provide a much greater understanding of agglomeration dynamics, mobility, and population responses to shocks. These advances promise to continue to enhance our understanding of distributional impacts related to trade (Redding 2020).

Governments now have numerous tools to support this analytical process. They increasingly use gender impact assessments, for example, to determine whether policy outcomes are likely to have differentiated outcomes for men and women (World Bank and WTO 2020). As demonstrated in the Sri Lanka case study in chapter 3, disaggregated analysis is also possible for the distributional outcomes between different regions within a country, across industries, and between high-skill and low-skill workers (Maliszewska, Osorio-Rodarte, and Gupta 2020). Such simulation exercises can make the process of developing complementary policies more proactive and data-driven and can also highlight trade-offs, such as when efficiency and equity objectives do not align.

Even so, there is a quite limited understanding of what works best in different national contexts. Despite a growing number of randomized experiments looking at the impacts of different complementary policies related to trade policy changes, this could still be much improved. Autor (2018, 9) argues that, in light of the advances in our understanding of the impacts of trade shocks on workers, firms, and communities, "it is incumbent on researchers and policy-makers to think creatively, rigorously, and experimentally … to discern what policies serve to maximize the shared gains from trade while minimizing the concentrated brunt of adjustment costs on a subset of citizens." Fortunately, we now have the tools in place to better predict the distributional impacts of reforms, depending on our knowledge of a country's economic characteristics. In this regard, the most productive areas for future work might be researching how solutions applied elsewhere could be successfully implemented in developing countries, especially low-income and fragile countries.

Take a whole-economy and whole-government lens to trade reforms
Given the large number of policy areas that relate to the distributional impacts of trade, there need to be institutional structures that accommodate cross-government coordination on trade reforms. One way to do this is by moving away from ministerial silos toward a focus on shared objectives. Doing so is likely to provide a better-informed and more inclusive process for trade negotiations while also creating the foundations for a policy framework that maximizes the gains from trade. In the process, it ensures that businesses can easily start up, FDI can enter, workers can easily move to expanding industries, and procedures to move goods to and across borders work efficiently. It can also allow for a preemptive bolstering of safety nets. Given the quite limited capacity for such coordinated approaches in many developing countries and the challenges of navigating the complex political economy of trade policy, external assistance to these processes and a gradualist approach to trade policy reform are often needed (Akman et al. 2019). In addition, the early announcement of policy changes can create a time cushion for workers to adjust their skills and transition to other industries (Hollweg et al. 2014).

Furthermore, there is a need to strongly engage the private sector and other non-governmental stakeholders (consumer groups and labor unions) in the reform process to better understand the nature of different distortions and potential risks. There is often a significant gap between de jure and de facto legal rules, especially in developing countries (Hallward-Driemeier and Pritchett 2015). Individuals who interact with the regulatory system daily are likely to better understand and identify what may limit the benefits from trade reforms. Establishing such processes is also essential for maintaining support throughout the many ups and downs of implementation. These lessons are informing the World Bank's approach to supporting the negotiations and eventual implementation on the African Continental Free Trade Area (box 4.2).

Providing a Solid Base for the African Continental Free Trade Area to Flourish

With 54 countries, the African Continental Free Trade Area (AfCFTA) will be the largest free trade area in the world in terms of membership, potentially covering a market of 1.3 billion people with a combined gross domestic product of US$3.4 trillion. Although free trade agreements (FTAs) create significant opportunities, history shows that maximizing their potential benefits is not automatic. A key issue is whether and how the AfCFTA institutions and member states address weaknesses that have limited the impact of previous regional FTAs in Africa.

To a great extent, the possibility that the AfCFTA will become a milestone for development in the region will depend on (a) the depth and breadth of detailed commitments to remove trade barriers that are to be negotiated, (b) the extent to which AfCFTA commitments are effectively implemented on the ground, and (c) complementary initiatives that ensure a smooth transition to free trade and induce greater flows of productive investment in nontraditional sectors, leading to more and better jobs.

As part of its engagement with the African Union, the World Bank has been helping AfCFTA stakeholders gather needed evidence to make informed decisions about the negotiation process over the past year. AfCFTA institutions and especially member states, many of which lack a track record on implementing the trade agreements they have signed, will continue to need additional support. The goal of that support is to effectively implement agreements, identify critical domestic bottlenecks, and prioritize actions to ensure a smooth transition to free trade and to attract more investment. It will thus be key to ensuring fairness and a level playing field for traders.

Drawing on the experience of similar negotiation exercises by other developing countries, we find that designing a complementary agenda to maximize the potential benefits of an FTA entails concrete actions on at least three fronts.

- *Implementation and administration of the AfCFTA agreement.* Capacity building (in the form of training, direct advice, and implementation support) benefits not only the ministries of trade but also other key ministries as well as border management agencies (especially customs) tasked with the future implementation of an agreement that they may previously have had only exposure to during the negotiation phase. This is essential to enable the compliance, administration and problem solving, economic monitoring, and socialization of the AfCFTA.
- *Trade-related institutional support for implementation.* Capacity building to agencies (other than the ministries of trade) that are in charge of trade and investment-related matters that in practice affect the correct functioning of the AfCFTA.
- *Transition to free trade.* Sector-specific initiatives aimed at enabling domestic firms (notably small and medium enterprises) to address economic distortions affecting competitiveness in a free-trade environment.

A Global Policy Agenda That Delivers for the Poor

Strengthen the effectiveness of the multilateral trade system

At a global level, defending the multilateral trading system is more essential than ever as the WTO faces growing challenges to its legitimacy (see Akman et al. 2018;

World Bank 2020). Such an effort will necessitate continued support to a rules-based system and a strengthening (and where needed, reform) of the WTO to increase its effectiveness in the context of rising protectionism. For a new WTO director general, this will mean tackling numerous urgent challenges with strong distributional implications such as resolving the crisis in the dispute settlement system, improving compliance, and resolving differences on special and differential treatment for developing countries (Fiorini et al. 2020).

What can be done to make the international system work better? Lowering trade barriers, notably in agriculture, would have a large impact on bringing greater gains from trade to the poorest. In the current pandemic, supporting multilateralism and international cooperation is particularly essential for ensuring a stable supply of medicine and food products, as well as supporting a robust recovery. There are also numerous areas beyond trade that require increased cooperation, including taxation, competition, state subsidies, and the regulation of international data flows (OECD 2017; World Bank 2020). Many of these were noted as national policy and regulatory priorities earlier in this chapter, but their integration into multilateral processes could enable agreement on certain baseline principles and minimum standards. Similarly, international cooperation in establishing and monitoring minimum labor standards and promoting responsible business conduct can improve conditions, especially for low-skill workers in developing countries (Hollweg 2019).

Address the trade-related impacts of exogenous shocks

As the spread of the COVID-19 pandemic has shown, exogenous shocks unrelated to trade can also have significant trade-related distributional impacts. The COVID-19 crisis hit service workers particularly hard, hindering the recovery of the trade in services (particularly travel and tourism) far more than that of merchandise trade (Ferrentino et al. 2020). In Bangladesh, workers in export sectors such as the apparel industry were affected by factory closures and wage losses, which affected female workers the most (Genoni et al. 2020). The aftermath of the current crisis is likely to result in a reshaping of GVCs to better manage risk, as well as potentially increasing the scale and scope of government intervention. Ensuring that the latter primarily addresses coordination failures rather than undermining openness and predictability will be essential. The poorest are particularly vulnerable when food value chains are disrupted and workers are unable to access inputs or to transport goods to market. This further increases the need to ensure that trade remains open, especially to expedite the flow of essential goods and services.

The pandemic is likely to increase the relevance of digital technologies in trade and augment the role of services. This has the potential to increase the gap between small and large firms and between advanced and low-income countries. It also creates opportunities for broad-based gains as lead firms realize the need to diversify their supplier base. It also could greatly decrease the cost of remoteness if investments in widely accessible and robust ICT systems are made. Furthermore, shorter supply chains may lead to greater regionalization and the development of more decentralized production and processing hubs connected through regional value chains.

In addressing the lasting impacts of the COVID-19 pandemic, it will be vital to boost the resilience of trade against the likely growing frequency of exogenous shocks, especially from climate change. Although attention is focused on reducing emissions, the climate is already changing, and solutions to both mitigate emissions and adapt to rising temperatures and more extreme weather events need to be identified now. The modes of how we trade—roads, rail, aviation, and sea transport—will be affected. Solutions could range from the need to redesign shipping containers and airport runways to the relocation and migration of people (Dellink et al. 2017). Country-specific interventions on trade liberalization could be better informed by an in-depth analysis of the nexus between international trade, climate change, and the prospects for the reduction of poverty and inequality. Trade-related interventions targeted at boosting agricultural productivity and consequently increasing farmer incomes could also put greater emphasis on the criticality of drought resiliency strategies (Alfani et al. 2019).

Conclusion

In sum, the discussion on better distributional outcomes in this chapter has focused on trade-related shocks, but many of the responses should be applicable to government responses to a broad variety of shocks. The post-1990 global integration of the Eastern bloc and in particular of China represented a macroeconomic event that was in many ways unique, and it is likely that the focus on trade adjustment in recent years is not representative for the coming decades (Akman et al. 2019). This also strengthens the case for thinking about adjustment costs and the need to improve distributional outcomes beyond trade-related shocks. As exogenous shocks unrelated to trade become more frequent, developing countries will need to continue strengthening their policy apparatus and economic foundations for resilient, competitive, and inclusive societies that can respond effectively to dislocation and adjustment.

Notes

1. The 2020 World Development Report, *Trading for Development in the Age of Global Value Chains* (World Bank 2020), distinguishes between approaches to supporting integration in countries that specialize in (a) agriculture and commodities to limited manufacturing, (b) limited manufacturing to advanced manufacturing and services, and (c) advanced manufacturing and services to innovative activities. Each stage requires that different policy priorities become more or less salient over time, depending on the stage of GVC participation.

2. As di Ubaldo and Winters (2019, p.1) note, "trade policy is not an employment policy and should not be expected to have major effects on overall employment [except where] it interacts with distortions in labor markets."

3. Moreover, the costs of adjustment on select industries and workers are often visible earlier than the highly diffused benefits from reforms experienced by consumers and exporting and importing firms. These distributional and temporal problems can lead to half-hearted implementation, reform reversals and dissuade policy makers from pursuing future efforts toward liberalization.

4. See, for example, Bas (2014) on India and Beverelli, Fiorini, and Hoekman (2017) for a sample of 56 countries at different stages of development.

5. Trade facilitation programs and policies can cover the full spectrum of border procedures, from the electronic exchange of data about a shipment, to the simplification and harmonization of trade documents and processes, to the implementation of measures to enhance transparency and predictability for traders.

6. McKenzie (2017) reviewed 24 randomized control trials. The one successful program focused on addressing spatial mismatches by providing young rural women in India with information about job opportunities in business process outsourcing (Jensen 2012).

References

Acemoglu, Daron, Asuman Ozdaglar, and Alireza Tahbaz-Salehi. 2015. "Systemic Risk and Stability in Financial Networks." *American Economic Review* 105 (2): 564–608.

Akman, Sait, Clara Brandi, Uri Dadush, Peter Draper, Andreas Freytag, Miriam Kaut, Peter Rashish, Johannes Schwarzer, and Rob Vos. 2018. "Mitigating the Adjustment Costs of International Trade." G20 Argentina: Trade, Investment and Tax Cooperation Task Force Brief. https://www .g20-insights.org/wp-content/uploads/2018/06/mitigating-the-adjustment-costs-of -international-trade-1529419478.pdf.

Akman, Sait, Shiro Armstrong, Carlos Primo Braga, Uri Dadush, Anabel Gonzalez, Fukunari Kimura, Junji Nagakawa, Peter Rashish, and Akihiko Tamura. 2019. "The Crisis in World Trade." Policy Brief, Policy Center for the New South. https://voxeu.org/content/crisis-world-trade.

Alfani, Federica, Aslihan Arslan, Nancy McCarthy, Romina Cavatassi, and Nicholas Sitko. 2019. "Climate Change Vulnerability in Rural Zambia: The Impact of an El Niño-Induced Shock on Income and Productivity." FAO Agricultural Development Economics Working Paper 2019/02. https://www.researchgate.net/publication/331248533_Climate-change_vulnerability_in _rural_Zambia_the_impact_of_an_El_Nino-induced_shock_on_income_and_productivity.

Alfaro-Ureña, Alonso, Isabela Manelici, and José P. Vásquez. 2019. "The Effects of Joining Multinational Supply Chains: New Evidence from Firm-to-Firm Linkages." *Supply Chain Management eJournal*. http://dx.doi.org/10.2139/ssrn.3376129.

Amiti, Mary, Mi Dai, Robert Feenstra, and John Romalis. 2017. "How Did China's WTO Entry Benefit US Consumers?" Staff Report 817, Federal Reserve Bank of New York. https://ideas.repec.org/p /fip/fednsr/817.html.

Amiti, Mary, and Joseph Konings. 2007. "Trade Liberalization, Intermediate Inputs, and Productivity: Evidence from Indonesia." *American Economic Review* 97 (5): 1611–38.

Anand, Rahul, and Purva Khera. 2016. "Macroeconomic Impact of Product and Labor Market Reforms on Informality and Unemployment in India." Working Paper 16/47, International Monetary Fund, Washington, DC.

Artuç, Erhan, Robert Cull, Susmita Dasgupta, Roberto Fattal, Deon Filmer, Xavier Giné, Hanan Jacoby, Dean Jolliffe, Hiau Looi Kee, Leora Klapper, Aart Kraay, Norman Loayza, David McKenzie, Berk Azler, Vijayendra Rao, Bob Rijkers, Sergio Schmukler, Michael Toman, Adam Wagstaff, and Michael Woolcock. 2020. "Toward Successful Development Policies: Insights from Research in Development Economics." Policy Research Working Paper 9133, World Bank, Washington, DC.

Artuç, Erhan, Daniel Lederman, and Guido Porto. 2015. "A Mapping of Labor Mobility Costs in the Developing World." *Journal of International Economics* 95 (1): 28–41.

Artuç, Erhan, Gladys Lopez-Acevedo, Raymond Robertson, and Daniel Samaan. 2019. *Exports to Jobs: Boosting the Gains from Trade in South Asia*. Washington, DC: World Bank.

Atkin, David, Dave Donaldson, Imran Rasul, Matthieu Teachout, Eric Verhoogen, and Christopher Woodruff. 2019. "Firms, Trade, and Productivity." International Growth Center Evidence Paper, London. https://www.theigc.org/wp-content/uploads/2019/12/IGC-Firms-evidence -paper-December-2019.pdf.

Autor, David. 2018. "Trade and Labor Markets: Lessons from China's Rise." *IZA World of Labor* (February): 431. https://wol.iza.org/uploads/articles/431/pdfs/trade-and-labor-makets-lessons -from-chinas-rise.pdf?v=1.

Bacchetta, Marc, Emmanuel Milet, and José-Antonio Monteiro. 2019. *Making Globalization More Inclusive: Lessons from Experience with Adjustment Policies*. Geneva: World Trade Organization.

Bacchetta, Marc, and Victor Stolzenburg. 2019. "Trade, Value Chains and Labor Markets in Advanced Economies." In *Global Value Chain Development Report 2019: Technological Innovation, Supply Chain Trade, and Workers in a Globalized World*, 45–61. Geneva: World Trade Organization. https://core.ac.uk/reader/288469718.

Banerjee, Abhijit V., and Esther Duflo. 2014. "Do Firms Want to Borrow More? Testing Credit Constraints Using a Directed Lending Program." *Review of Economic Studies* 81 (2): 572–607.

Bas, Maria. 2014. "Does Services Liberalization Affect Manufacturing Firms' Export Performance? Evidence from India." *Journal of Comparative Economics* 42 (3): 569–89.

Bastos, Paul, and Nicolas Santos. Forthcoming. "Long-Run Effects of Trade Liberalization on Regional Dynamics: Evidence from South Africa." World Bank, Washington, DC.

Belghazi, Saad, and Kawthar Berbich. 2019. "The Policy to Mitigate the Effects of the 2008 Global Crisis on Textile, Clothing, Leather and Footwear Jobs in Morocco." In *Making Globalization More Inclusive*, edited by Marc Bacchetta, Emmanuel Milet, and José-Antonio Monteiro. Geneva: World Trade Organization.

Beverelli, Cosimo, Matteo Fiorini, and Bernard Hoekman. 2017. "Services Trade Policy and Manufacturing Productivity: The Role of Institutions." *Journal of International Economics* 104 (C): 166–82.

Beverelli, Cosimo, Alexander Keck, Mario Larch, and Yoto Yotov. 2018. "Institutions, Trade, and Development: A Quantitative Analysis." CESifo Working Paper 6920, Center for Economic Studies and ifo Institute (CESifo), Munich, Germany.

Bloom, Nicholas, and John van Reenen. 2010. "Why Do Management Practices Differ across Firms and Countries?" *Journal of Economic Perspectives* 24 (1): 203–24.

Bosch, Mariano, Edwin Goñi-Pacchioni, and William Maloney. 2012. "Trade Liberalization, Labor Reforms, and Formal–Informal Employment Dynamics." *Labor Economics* 19 (5): 653–67.

Busso, Matias, and Sebastian Galiani. 2019. "The Causal Effect of Competition on Prices and Quality: Evidence from a Field Experiment." *American Economic Journal: Applied Economics* 11 (1): 33–56.

Cadot, Olivier, Ana Fernandes, Julien Gourdon, and Aaditya Mattoo. 2015. "Are the Benefits of Export Support Durable? Evidence from Tunisia." *Journal of International Economics* 97 (2): 310–24.

Calì, Massimiliano, Taufik Hidayat, and Claire Hollweg. 2019. "What Is Behind Labor Mobility Costs? Evidence from Indonesia." Background Paper for the Urbanization Flagship Report, World Bank, Washington, DC. https://openknowledge.worldbank.org/handle/10986/32458.

Campante, Filipe, and David Yanagizawa-Drott. 2018. "Long-Range Growth: Economic Development in the Global Network of Air Links." *Quarterly Journal of Economics* 133 (3): 1395–458.

Card, David, Jochen Kluve, and Andrea Weber. 2018. "What Works? A Meta-Analysis of Recent Active Labor Market Program Evaluations." *Journal of the European Economic Association* 16 (3): 894–931.

Carvalho, Vasco, and Alireza Tahbaz-Salehi. 2019. "Production Networks: A Primer." *Annual Review of Economics* 11: 635–63.

Chalendard, Cyril, Alice Duhaut, Ana M. Fernandes, Aaditya Mattoo, Gael Raballand, and Bob Rijkers. 2020. "Does Better Information Curb Customs Fraud?" Policy Research Working Paper 9254, World Bank, Washington, DC.

Chang, Roberto, Linda Kaltani, and Norman Loayza. 2009. "Openness Can Be Good for Growth: The Role of Policy Complementarities." *Journal of Development Economics* 90 (1): 33–49.

Charlot, Olivier, Franck Malherbet, and Cristina Terra. 2015. "Informality in Developing Economies: Regulation and Fiscal Policies." *Journal of Economic Dynamics and Control* 51: 1–27.

Cirera, Xavier, and William F. Maloney. 2017. *The Innovation Paradox: Developing Country Capabilities and the Unrealized Promise of Technological Catch-Up*. Washington, DC: World Bank. https://openknowledge.worldbank.org/handle/10986/28341.

Cirera, Xavier, Dirk Willenbockel, and Rajith W. D. Lakshman. 2014. "Evidence on the Impact of Tariff Reductions on Employment in Developing Countries: A Systematic Review." *Journal of Economic Surveys* 28 (3): 449–71.

Clemens, Michael A. 2011. "Economics and Emigration: Trillion Dollar Bills on the Sidewalk?" *Journal of Economic Perspectives* 25 (3): 83–106.

Colantone, Italo, and Rosario Crinò. 2014. "New Imported Inputs, New Domestic Products." *Journal of International Economics* 92 (1): 147–65.

Cutler, Wendy, and Jacob Bell. 2018. "Adjusting to Trade: Asia-Pacific Approaches to Assisting Displaced Workers." Asia Society Policy Institute. https://asiasociety.org/sites/default/files/2018-04/Trade%20Adjustment%20Paper%20FINAL.pdf.

Czubala, Witold, Ben Shepherd, and John S. Wilson. 2009. "Help or Hindrance? The Impact of Harmonized Standards on African Exports." *Journal of African Economies* 18 (5): 711–44.

Dauda, Seidu. 2020. *The Effects of Competition on Jobs and Economic Transformation. EFI Insight-Trade, Investment and Competitiveness*. Washington, DC: World Bank.

Dellink, Rob, Hyunjeong Hwang, Elisa Lanzi, and Jean Chateau. 2017. "International Trade Consequences of Climate Change." OECD Trade and Environment Working Paper 2017/01, Organisation for Economic Co-operation and Development, Paris.

Depetris-Chauvin, Nicolás, Pablo Depetris-Chauvin, and Francis Mulangu. 2017. "The Poverty Impact of Modernising Dar es Salaam Port." In *Trade and Poverty Reduction: New Evidence of Impacts in Developing Countries*. Geneva: World Trade Organization.

De Soyres, François, and Alexandre Gaillard. 2019. "Trade, Global Value Chains and GDP Comovement: An Empirical Investigation." Policy Research Working Paper 9091, World Bank, Washington, DC.

Díaz, Juan José, and David Rosas-Shady. 2016. "Impact Evaluation of the Job Youth Training Program Projoven." Working Paper IDB-WP-693, Inter-American Development Bank, Washington, DC.

Disdier, Anne-Celia, Lionel Fontagné, and Olivier Cadot. 2015. "North-South Standards Harmonization and International Trade." *World Bank Economic Review* 29 (2): 327–52.

Di Ubaldo, Mattia, and L. Alan Winters. 2020. "International Trade Regulation and Job Creation." *IZA World of Labor* (February): 1–75.

Dix-Carneiro, Rafael, Pinelopi K. Goldberg, Costas Meghir, and Gabriel Ulyssea. 2021. "Trade and Informality in the Presence of Labor Market Frictions and Regulations." Working Paper 28391, National Bureau of Economic Research, Cambridge, MA.

Donaldson, Dave. 2018. "Railroads of the Raj: Estimating the Impact of Transportation Infrastructure." *American Economic Review* 108 (4–5): 899–934.

Echandi, Roberto, Jana Krajcovicova, and Christine Z. Qiang. 2015. "The Impact of Investment Policy in a Changing Global Economy: A Review of the Literature." Policy Research Working Paper 7437, World Bank, Washington, DC.

Escudero, Veronica, Kochen Kluve, Elva López Mourelo, and Clemente Pignatti. 2019. "Active Labor Market Programs in Latin America and the Caribbean: Evidence from a Meta-Analysis." *Journal of Development Studies* 55 (12): 2644–61.

Fafchamps, Marcel, David McKenzie, Simon Quinn, and Christopher Woodruff. 2014. "Microenterprise Growth and the Flypaper Effect: Evidence from a Randomized Experiment in Ghana." *Journal of Development Economics* 106: 211–26.

Fafchamps, Marcel, and Simon Quinn. 2018. "Networks and Manufacturing Firms in Africa: Results from a Randomized Field Experiment." *World Bank Economic Review* 32 (3): 656–75.

Fajgelbaum, Pablo, and Stephen Redding. 2018. "Trade, Structural Transformation and Development: Evidence from Argentina 1869–1914." Working Paper 20217, National Bureau of Economic Research, Cambridge, MA.

Farole, Thomas, and Deborah Winkler, eds. 2014. *Making Foreign Direct Investment Work for Sub-Saharan Africa: Local Spillovers and Competitiveness in Global Value Chains.* Washington, DC: World Bank.

Fernandes, Ana, Esteban Ferro, and John Wilson. 2019. "Product Standards and Firms' Export Decisions." *World Bank Economic Review* 33 (2): 353–74.

Fernandes, Ana, Aaditya Mattoo, Huy Nguyen, and Marc Schiffbauer. 2019. "The Internet and Chinese Exports in the Pre-Ali Baba Era." *Journal of Development Economics* 138 (C): 57–76.

Fernando, A. Nilesh. 2020. "Shackled to the Soil? Inherited Land, Birth Order, and Labor Mobility." *Journal of Human Resources*, online preprint version. http://jhr.uwpress.org/content /early/2020/02/03/jhr.57.2.0219-10014R2.abstract.

Ferrentino, Michael, Jean-François Arvis, Paul Brenton, Cristina Constantinescu, Karlygash Dairabayeva, Ian Gillson, Karen Muramatsu, and Daria Ulybina. 2020. "Shipping Signals Flattening Trade." COVID-19 Trade Watch 8, World Bank, Washington, DC.

Fiorini, Matteo, Bernard Hoekman, Petros C. Mavroidis, Douglas Nelson, and Robert Wolfe. 2020. "Stakeholder Preferences and Priorities for the Next WTO Director General." Research Paper RSCAS 43, Robert Schuman Center for Advanced Studies, Florence, Italy.

Freund, Caroline, and Bineswaree Bolaky. 2008. "Trade, Regulations, and Income." *Journal of Development Economics* 87 (2): 309–21.

Freund, Caroline, and Nadia Rocha. 2011. "What Constrains Africa's Exports?" *World Bank Economic Review* 25 (3): 361–86.

Fuglie, Keith, Madhur Gauta, Aparajita Goyal, and William Maloney. 2019. *Harvesting Prosperity: Technology and Productivity Growth in Agriculture.* Washington, DC: World Bank.

Genoni, Maria Eugenia, Afsana Iffat Khan, Nandini Krishnan, Nethra Palaniswamy, and Wameq Raza. 2020. "Losing Livelihoods: The Labor Market Impacts of COVID-19 in Bangladesh." Working paper, World Bank, Washington, DC.

Ghose, Devaki. 2019. "Trade, Internal Migration, and Human Capital: Who Gains from India's IT Boom?" Graduate thesis, University of Virginia, Charlottesville.

Grossman, Gene, and Elhanan Helpman. 1994. "Endogenous Innovation in the Theory of Growth." *Journal of Economic Perspectives* 8 (1): 23–44.

G20 Research Group. 2017. "G20 Leaders' Declaration: Shaping an Interconnected World." Hamburg, Germany, July 8. http://www.g20.utoronto.ca/2017/2017-G20-leaders-declaration.html.

Hallward-Driemeier, Mary, and Lant Pritchett. 2015. "How Business Is Done in the Developing World: Deals versus Rules." *Journal of Economic Perspectives* 29 (3): 121–40.

Hirshleifer, Sarojini, David McKenzie, Rita Almeida, and Cristobal Ridao-Cano. 2016. "The Impact of Vocational Training for the Unemployed: Experimental Evidence from Turkey." *Economic Journal* 126 (597: 2115–46.

Hoekman, Bernard, and Douglas Nelson. 2019. "How Should We Think about the Winners and Losers from Globalization? A Reply to Nicolas Lamp." *European Journal of International Law* 30 (4): 1399–408.

Hollweg, Claire. 2019. "Firm Compliance and Public Disclosure in Vietnam." Policy Research Working Paper 9026, World Bank, Washington, DC.

Hollweg, Claire, Daniel Lederman, Diego Rojas, and Elizabeth Ruppert Bulmer. 2014. *Sticky Feet: How Labor Market Frictions Shape the Impact of International Trade on Jobs and Wages*. Washington, DC: World Bank.

Huneeus, Federico. 2018. "Production Network Dynamics and the Propagation of Shocks." Graduate thesis, Princeton University, Princeton, NJ.

Iacovone, Leonardo, Ferdinand Rauch, and L. Alan Winters. 2013. "Trade as an Engine of Creative Destruction: Mexican Experience with Chinese Competition." *Journal of International Economics* 89 (2): 379–92.

Ibarrarán, Pablo, and David Rosas-Shady. 2009. "Evaluating the Impact of Job Training Programs in Latin America: Evidence from IDB Funded Operations." *Journal of Development Effectiveness* 1 (2): 195–216.

ILO (International Labour Organization). 2013. *Comparative Review of Unemployment and Employment Insurance Experiences in Asia and Worldwide*. Geneva: ILO.

IMF (International Monetary Fund), World Bank, and WTO (World Trade Organization). 2017. *Making Trade an Engine of Growth for All: The Case for Trade and for Policies to Facilitate Adjustment*. Washington, DC: International Monetary Fund. https://www.imf.org/en /Publications/Policy-Papers/Issues/2017/04/08/making-trade-an-engine-of-growth-for-all.

Irwin, Douglas A. 2019. "Does Trade Reform Promote Economic Growth? A Review of Recent Evidence." Working Paper 25927, National Bureau of Economic Research, Cambridge, MA.

Jensen, Robert. 2012. "Do Labor Market Opportunities Affect Young Women's Work and Family Decisions? Experimental Evidence from India." *Quarterly Journal of Economics* 127 (2): 753–92.

Kusek, Peter, and Andrea Silva. 2018. "What Investors Want: Perceptions and Experiences of Multinational Corporations in Developing Countries." Policy Research Working Paper 8383, World Bank, Washington, DC.

Lagakos, David. 2020. "Urban-Rural Gaps in the Developing World: Does Internal Migration Offer Opportunities?" *Journal of Economic Perspectives* 34 (3): 174–92.

Lake, James, and Daniel Millimet. 2016. "An Empirical Analysis of Trade-Related Redistribution and the Political Viability of Free Trade." *Journal of International Economics* 99 (C): 156–78.

Lederman, Daniel, Gladys Lopez-Acevedo, and Yevgeniya Savchenko. 2014. "Trade Adjustment Assistance Programs." World Bank, Washington, DC.

Lee, Eunhee, and Kei Mu Yi. 2018. "Global Value Chains and Inequality with Endogenous Labor Supply." *Journal of International Economics* 115: 223–41.

Lee, Vicky. 2000 "Unemployment Insurance and Assistance Systems in Mainland China." Hong Kong Legislative Council Secretariat, Hong Kong SAR, China.

Lopez-Acevedo, Gladys, Denis Medvedev, and Vincent Palmade. 2017. *South Asia's Turn: Policies to Boost Competitiveness and Create the Next Export Powerhouse*. Washington, DC: World Bank.

Maliszewska, Maryla, Israel Osorio-Rodarte, and Rakesh Gupta. 2020. "Ex Ante Evaluation of Subnational Labor Market Impacts of Trade Reforms." Policy Research Working Paper 9478, World Bank, Washington, DC.

Martínez Licetti, Martha, Mariana Iootty, Tanja Goodwin, and José Signoret. 2018. *Strengthening Argentina's Integration into the Global Economy: Policy Proposals for Trade, Investment, and Competition*. Washington, DC: World Bank.

Mattoo, Aditya, Nadia Rocha, and Michele Ruta. 2020. "The Evolution of Deep Trade Agreements." Policy Research Working Paper 9283, World Bank, Washington, DC.

McCaig, Brian, and Nina Pavcnik. 2018. "Export Markets and Labor Allocation in a Low-Income Country." *American Economic Review* 108 (7): 1899–941.

McKenzie, David. 2017. "How Effective Are Active Labor Market Policies in Developing Countries? A Critical Review of Recent Evidence." *World Bank Research Observer* 32 (2): 127–54.

McKenzie, David, and Christopher Woodruff. 2017. "Business Practices in Small Firms in Developing Countries." Policy Research Working Paper 7405, World Bank, Washington, DC.

Munshi, Kaivan, and Mark Rosenzweig. 2016. "Networks and Misallocation: Insurance, Migration, and the Rural-Urban Wage Gap." *American Economic Review* 106 (1): 46–98.

Ngo, Thi. 2016. "Unemployment Insurance in Viet Nam: Challenges and Adjustments." United Nations Economic Commission for Asia and the Pacific, Bangkok.

Nordås, Hildegunn K., and Roberta Piermartini. 2004. "Infrastructure and Trade." Staff Working Paper ERSD-2004-04, World Trade Organization, Geneva.

OECD (Organisation for Economic Co-operation and Development). 2017. "Making Trade Work for All." OECD Trade Policy Paper 202, OECD, Paris.

Ohno, Kenichi. 2009. "Avoiding the Middle-Income Trap: Renovating Industrial Policy Formulation in Vietnam." *ASEAN Economic Bulletin* 26 (1): 25–43.

Qiang, Christine Z., and Ryan Kuo. 2020. "Supporting Informal Businesses amid COVID-19 without Formalization." *Private Sector Development Blog*, December 16, 2020. https://blogs.worldbank .org/psd/supporting-informal-businesses-amid-covid-19-without-formalization.

Qiang, Christine Z., Yan Liu, and Victor Steenbergen. 2021. *Global Value Chains: An Investment Perspective*. Washington, DC: World Bank.

Paravisini, Daniel, Veronica Rappoport, Philipp Schnabl, and Daniel Wolfenzon. 2015. "Dissecting the Effect of Credit Supply on Trade: Evidence from Matched Credit-Export Data." *Review of Economic Studies*, 82 (1), 333–59.

Redding, Stephen J. 2020. "Trade and Geography." Working Paper 27821, National Bureau of Economic Research, Cambridge, MA.

Robertson, Raymond, Deeksha Kokas, Diego Cardozo, and Gladys Lopez-Acevedo. 2020. "Short- and Long-Run Labor Market Effects of Developing Country Exports: Evidence from Bangladesh. Discussion Paper 13041, Institute of Labor Economics (IZA), Bonn, Germany.

Rodriguez, Francisco, and Dani Rodrik. 1999. "Trade Policy and Economic Growth: A Skeptic's Guide to the Cross-National Evidence." *NBER Macroeconomics Annual* 15: 261–325.

Rodríguez-Castelán, Carlos, Emmanuel Vazquez, and Hernan Winkler. 2020. "Tracing the Local Impacts of Exports on Poverty and Inequality in Mexico." Discussion Paper 13610, Institute of Labor Economics (IZA), Bonn, Germany.

Rodrik, Dani. 2018. "What Do Trade Agreements Really Do?" *Journal of Economic Perspectives* 32 (2): 73–90.

Rodrik, Dani. 2020. "Why Does Globalization Fuel Populism? Economics, Culture, and the Rise of Rightwing Populism." Working Paper 27526, National Bureau of Economic Research, Cambridge, MA.

Sáez, Sebastián, ed. 2013. *Let Workers Move: Using Bilateral Labor Agreements to Increase Trade in Services*. Washington, DC: World Bank.

Sequeira, Sandra, and Simeon Djankov. 2014. "Corruption and Firm Behavior: Evidence from African Ports." *Journal of International Economics* 94 (2): 277–94.

Topalova, Petia, and Amit Khandelwal. 2011. "Trade Liberalization and Firm Productivity: The Case of India." *Review of Economics and Statistics* 93 (3): 995–1009.

Wacziarg, Romain, and Karen H. Welch. 2008. "Trade Liberalization and Growth: New Evidence." *World Bank Economic Review* 22 (2): 187–231.

World Bank. 2017. *In Bangladesh, Empowering and Employing Women in the Garments Sector*. Washington, DC: World Bank.

World Bank. 2019. *World Development Report 2019: The Changing Nature of Work*. Washington, DC: World Bank.

World Bank. 2020a. *The African Continental Free Trade Agreement: Economic and Distributional Effects.* Washington, DC: World Bank.

World Bank. 2020b. *World Development Report 2020: Trading for Development in the Age of Global Value Chains.* Washington, DC: World Bank.

World Bank. 2021. *World Development Report 2021: Data for Better Lives.* Washington, DC: World Bank.

World Bank and WTO (World Trade Organization). 2015. *The Role of Trade in Ending Poverty.* Geneva: WTO.

World Bank and WTO (World Trade Organization). 2020. *Women and Trade: The Role of Trade in Promoting Gender Equality.* Washington, DC: World Bank.

Zi, Yuan. 2016. "Trade Liberalization and the Great Labor Reallocation." Graduate Institute of International and Development Studies Working Paper 18-2016, Graduate Institute of International and Development Studies, Geneva.

Appendix A. Methodological Approaches Applied in the Case Studies

The methodological approaches applied in this report are complementary. The backward-looking analysis assesses the importance of various channels of the impact of trade changes on employment, wages, informality across time, regions, and demographic characteristics such as age and skill level. The Household Impact of Tariffs (HIT) methodology captures ex ante short-term impacts of tariff liberalization and allows for granularity of outcomes across households given changes in tariffs at the product level. It incorporates detailed consumption patterns at the household level and is best equipped to estimate short-term impacts on consumption. The Computable General Equilibrium–Global Income Distribution Dynamics (CGE-GIDD) approach allows for the ex ante medium- and long-term assessment of the impacts of trade policy reforms because the model includes input-output relationships across sectors, differences across countries in the sectoral compositions of their economies, and bilateral trade relationships. It also imposes economic consistency because changes across all variables add up to the total productive capacity within the economy consistent with factors of production and sectoral productivity. The impacts on households and regions are generated in microsimulations consistent with the aggregate shocks.

Overall, the HIT approach is more restrictive but provides very detailed results, whereas the CGE-GIDD approach is more flexible but requires more data and provides results aggregated at the sectoral level. The two approaches are likely to be broadly consistent in terms of their impacts on household consumption, as illustrated by the Sri Lanka policy simulations in table A.1. At the same time, both approaches lack the richness of the impacts of trade policy shocks on the type of employment, wages for formal and informal workers, and the different types of occupation that are covered in the ex post analysis.

TABLE A.1 Methodological Approaches Applied in the Case Studies

	Ex post analysis	Ex ante short-term analysis HIT	Ex ante medium- and long-term analysis CGE-GIDD
Main purpose	Assess the short- and long-run response of local and regional labor market employment and wages to a greater exposure to trade.	Assess the first-order short-term distributional impacts of trade policy changes.	Assess medium- to long-term implications of comprehensive trade policy reforms that affect the economy as a whole and where second-order effects through input-output linkages are likely to be significant.
Questions that can be addressed with the methodology	▪ What are the channels through which trade affects local poverty rates and labor market dynamics? ▪ What are the effects that trade exerts through wage differentials and job opportunities across industries, occupations, and regions on the welfare of workers? ▪ How big are the mobility costs related to labor or capital? ▪ Which policy interventions are associated with better local socioeconomic outcomes?	▪ What are the aggregate gains in welfare from changes in tariffs and other import taxes? ▪ How are these gains distributed across households? ▪ To what extent do these gains reflect consumption gains or income losses?	▪ What are the potential impacts of trade policy changes (tariffs, nontariff measures, trade facilitation reforms, regulatory barriers in services) on macroeconomic aggregates such as economic growth and international trade? ▪ What are the impacts on poverty and the income distribution? ▪ What are the impacts on wages and employment of skilled/unskilled and female/male workers at the sectoral and subnational levels?
Overview of methodology and key assumptions	Partial equilibrium approach. Impacts of trade on local labor markets within the same country may differ because of differences in their initial sectoral composition and are thus not equally exposed to nationwide sectoral changes in trade exposure. Assumptions: (a) highly concentrated or localized production and (b) the existence of adjustment costs that limit the mobility of workers across regions.	Partial equilibrium approach. Households in different parts of the income distribution consume different goods and derive their income from different sources. Price changes resulting from a change in tariffs will affect different households differently. When tariffs are reduced (increased), households typically face lower (higher) prices for consumption goods, but they may also face a reduction (increase) in their incomes when they are selling such goods. The overall impact on a given household is the sum of the product-specific impacts. Assumptions: shocks to tariffs are fully transmitted to changes in prices faced by households and their wages.	General equilibrium approach combined with microsimulations. Trade policy changes lead to changes in comparative advantage across sectors and countries affecting bilateral sectoral trade and output patterns in line with the availability of factors of production and technological capabilities. The resulting changes in household income, employment, and wages are transferred as shocks to microsimulations. Assumptions: (a) demographics and education evolve in line with UN projections, (b) labor mobile across sectors with flexible wages, (c) investment endogenous with capital semi-mobile, (d) fixed trade balance, (e) exogenous unemployment, and (f) fixed government expenditures.

(Table continues on the following page.)

The Distributional Impacts of Trade

	Ex post analysis	Ex ante short-term analysis HIT	Ex ante medium- and long-term analysis CGE-GIDD
Data requirements	▣ Detailed labor force survey data representative at regional level covering wages, employment, and informality. ▣ Demographic characteristics (such as gender, location, and skills) to study distributional impacts. ▣ Labor force data matched to detailed trade data from UN Comtrade or national sources.	▣ Household survey data matched with trade policy data. ▣ Detailed data on household expenditures and income sources derived from representative household surveys harmonized with tariff data from TRAINS. ▣ The average budget and income shares across households in that percentile available for each of the 53 products covered.	▣ Global Trade Analysis Project database including globally consistent set of social accounting matrixes covering 121 countries and 65 sectors. ▣ Harmonized household survey data in World Bank collections (128 countries).
Type of outputs	▣ Estimates capture differential impacts of changes in trade (depending on trade exposure across regions) on labor outcomes. ▣ This geography-based methodology identifies only the region-specific part of changes in labor outcomes and not the aggregate effect; therefore, the estimated impact is the lower bound of the actual impact.	▣ Estimates of changes in consumption and (real) income at household level. ▣ Aggregate gains from trade policy changes and their impact on inequality and poverty. ▣ The tool available on the HIT external website.	Baseline evolution up to 2035 and scenario deviations from the baseline of the following: ▣ Growth, trade, and sectoral output. ▣ Wages and employment of workers (disaggregated by skill, gender, and region), and two-digit level of economic classification. ▣ Inequality and poverty estimates. ▣ Maps with subnational impacts on employment shifts.
Caveats	▣ The approach captures only differential effects across districts. ▣ It captures dynamic gains from trade.	▣ The approach does not quantify general equilibrium effects and modeling adjustment dynamics, which may be very important, especially in the longer run, because doing so would require a different set of modeling assumptions.	▣ The approach fails to capture the adjustment path and implementation costs of policy changes. ▣ Dynamic gains from trade are not fully represented, and technological progress is exogenous.
Policy recommendations	Promotes understanding around which channels of impact (such as employment, wages, and informality) are more prominent, given a trade shock across region, time, and demographic characteristics (such as age and skill level). More complex analysis can account for mobility costs and adjustment mechanisms.	Quantifies winners and losers across households. The limit on disaggregation is on household survey sampling. It can be decomposed by demographic and geographic characteristics.	Guide on sequencing of reforms, given the overall growth impacts and poverty reduction. Identify winners and losers from policy changes at the sectoral, subnational, and household level by skill, gender, occupation, and location to assist formulation of policies to minimize the adjustment costs.

Source: World Bank.

Note: CGE-GIDD = Computable General Equilibrium–Global Income Distribution Dynamics; HIT = Household Impact of Tariffs; TRAINS = Trade Analysis Information System; UN = United Nations.